with ... regards

from

[signature]

7 50

presentation

ALBERT SCHWEITZER

by Albert Schweitzer

CHRISTIANITY AND THE RELIGIONS
OF THE WORLD
MEMOIRS OF CHILDHOOD AND YOUTH
MY LIFE AND THOUGHT
FROM MY AFRICAN NOTEBOOK

ALBERT SCHWEITZER

A STUDY OF HIS PHILOSOPHY OF LIFE

BY

GABRIEL LANGFELDT

*Translated from the Norwegian
by Maurice Michael*

Ruskin House

GEORGE ALLEN & UNWIN LTD

MUSEUM STREET LONDON

Translated from ALBERT SCHWEITZER
published by
H. Aschehoug & Co. (W. Nygaard) Oslo, 1958

PRINTED IN GREAT BRITAIN
in 11 *on* 12 *pt Georgian type*
BY THE BLACKFRIARS PRESS LTD
LEICESTER

CONTENTS

INTRODUCTION TO THE
NORWEGIAN EDITION

AFTER all that has been written by and about Albert Schweitzer it might seem superfluous to publish another book on certain aspects of his philosophy. Yet, the public discussion that followed Schweitzer's visit to Norway, which my newspaper articles and the ecclesiastical controversy over Bishop Kristian Schjelderup further stimulated, revealed such a difference of ideas about Schweitzer's attitude to the concept of God and the basis of ethics in particular, that a more detailed analysis of this would seem to be called for. On the one hand, some of our theologians wanted to use Schweitzer to support the orthodox Christian view of God, while others expelled him from the community of Christians in a manner that has not been without offence. This public discussion revealed the fact that many who spoke with the assurance of familiarity with Albert Schweitzer's philosophy cannot have studied it deeply enough. Without thoroughly examining the implication of the concepts, they had simply assumed that when Schweitzer, for example, uses the expression God, he means by that an abstraction in the form of a personal divinity, and that when he mentions assembling his patients in Lambarene for *prayer*, he uses the word in the same way as practising Christians do. If, however, one studies what Schweitzer himself has written, one will soon realize that his concept of God and his whole view of man and the purpose of existence diverge so radically from the dogmatic view of Christianity held in Norway, that it is understandable that the question of whether or not he can be regarded as a Christian can be looked at from a number of different angles, both theological and philosophical.

As we shall see, he has broken so radically with the Christian confession that he says *inter alia* that *the only thing necessary* in order to be in harmony with the purpose of life is to follow the will-to-live and to practise *love*.

*

The ecclesiastical controversy we have recently witnessed in Norway has revealed narrow-mindedness, intolerance and slavish literalism as the chief characteristics of a large section of the clergy and of many of our congregational councils. Schweitzer, with his insistence on truth, his tolerance and broadmindedness stands out as a shining light compared with whom many of our prelates pale.

If one takes into consideration his endeavour to follow in Jesus' footsteps and what he has done in the service of mankind, and if by Christian is meant a person who is filled with the spirit of loving kindness, then he is a better Christian than most who pride themselves on being Christians.

That I have felt impelled to illumine certain aspects of Schweitzer's philosophy was not in the first place in order to substantiate the above; but in order, in doing so, to stress Schweitzer's message that if the world is not to march on to destruction, there must be a renewal of the use of thinking both in religion and ethics. The days of the dogma-ridden Christian confession are numbered, and therefore the Christian countries will have to undergo a new reformation and thereby arrive at the one true gospel of Christianity, that of love.

Because, in the first place, I can go with Schweitzer a long way where his views of life's problems is concerned and also because I believe that here he has a message for all who have come up against the same difficulties over subscribing to the official Christian doctrine, I hope that the following will be of interest. To formulate Schweitzer's philosophy in clearly defined views is certainly not easy. As several writers have pointed out, there is a peculiar dualism in him which betrays the fact that for all his strong emphasis on the importance of rational thinking, irrational forces also play a dominating part. What makes Schweitzer's philosophy distinctive and individual, however, is just this fact that he is an agnostic in his philosophy of life, yet lets his thinking stop and becomes an *ethical mystic* when faced with the miracle as it is manifested in man as the *will-to-live* and *reverence for life*.

The presence of the qualities underlying Schweitzer's life-view can be observed very early in the development of his personality, and to that extent one can say that he was predestined by Nature to stand out well above the average, especially where basic moral attributes are concerned. But it is equally certain that his great model has been Jesus Christ and it is possible in all sorts of ways to see how he has striven to resemble him. Even though Schweitzer had plenty of good models to follow both in Christendom and in the good Christian milieu in which he grew up, it is remarkable, as one can see so clearly from his little autobiography *Memoirs of Childhood and Youth*,[1] how the ethical sides of his personality developed with inner power each time that some event provoked his sensitive mind to identification and made him feel

[1] London: George Allen & Unwin.

responsible for his fellow creatures. I know of no other book that more convincingly proves how an aptitude to develop ethics and morals has biological roots nor one that so instructively demonstrates how moral reactions regularly are the result of the purely human urge to sympathize with and identify oneself with other creatures, without it being necessary to assume the existence of a moral code. *Memoirs of Childhood and Youth* can provide an excellent point of departure for understanding both Schweitzer's attitude to the question of the basis of morality and his view of humanity as a whole. But the reader must draw the more concrete conclusions himself. It is typical that Schweitzer seldom provides a clear philosophic formulation of his views. That, probably, is also why people's opinions of him have proved so different over this question of ethics and his attitude to Christianity. That this is so, is probably due in part to a certain shyness about revealing his inmost opinions. This inhibition applied not only to revealing what he had experienced in a beautiful piece of music, but in the same way as he had the profoundest respect for other people's intellectual life—he considered a mental analysis of others inadmissible unless for some special purpose—it is obvious that he is reluctant to reveal secrets that he considers to be no concern of others. Because of this, *Memoirs of Childhood and Youth* is not frank in the normal meaning of the word. There are many sides to his personality that remain veiled and unelucidated. But the remarkable thing is that even with views, about which one would think it more or less natural to be explicit, it is often only by indirect conclusion that the reader can arrive at what Schweitzer actually accepts. As has already been said, this applies to the *concept of God*. One would have thought it would have been natural for Schweitzer to explain in more or less unambiguous terms whether or not he believed in a *personal* God who intervenes in the ordering of the world and is responsible for the fate of the individual, and whether he thinks that *prayers* are heard. Yet in his books there is nothing at all precise about these two important points. On the other hand, we can conclude *indirectly* that he considers it vain to occupy oneself with such problems; for where the world-view is concerned—that is, the view of all the problems that rear their heads when we try to understand every-thing in the outside world—he declares himself an *agnostic*. Thus it follows that one must be correct in concluding, *inter alia,* that he considers there to be no proof that God intervenes in the fate of the individual person or that it is God who is responsible for all the unhappiness and misery in the world. In other words, a point of view very divergent from the usual Christian view that everything that happens is an expression of God's will. In 'He that loses his life shall find it' in *Moral Principles of Action* and elsewhere, he expresses himself very clearly in so far as he says emphatically that a faith rooted in an abstraction, in the absolute, is just a dead religion, and it is evident that he advocates the idea that *the Kingdom of God is within us.* Yet it is just on this point that problems arise when one tries to evaluate Schweitzer's philosophy from the purely rational point of view. It is, for example, difficult to understand Schweitzer ever holding services with prayer and the usual ceremonial as he has described himself doing in Lambarene. What is the purpose of prayer, if it is not directed to a transcendental Divinity who can be

13

envisaged as hearing it and possibly granting it? It was this and other indications of dualism that induced me to try and make a closer analysis of Schweitzer's views of ethics and religion. The correspondence I conducted during 1956 and 1957 with Schweitzer personally enables me to feel that I have got to the bottom of his views on these problems and also has confirmed the views I had already formed after studying his own writings. I have Schweitzer's permission to impart the thought and ideas contained in these letters and I shall come back to this later.[1]

Let us first take a brief look at Schweitzer's childhood and upbringing, paying special attention to the factors that were significant for the development of his views on ethics and morality. Then let us discuss the life-view for which he stands, using as a basis his own writings and the opinions of him of other authors, and, finally, consider against the background of the evidence, whether he can be labelled as a representative of any known philosophic or religious system.

[1] That the content of Schweitzer's letters is not given by direct quotation is because, in one of his letters, Schweitzer requested that if I wanted to publish the content of his letters, I should use my own words to do so, just giving their import. The reason for this request is that he would prefer to address himself to the reading public in his own way that is fitted to the problems at hand. Because of this request, I have quoted him verbatim only exceptionally and otherwise just communicated the thoughts and ideas contained in the letters. It has not proved necessary to quote much from these letters, as most of what they contain is also to be found in his writings from which I have quoted verbatim.

INTRODUCTION TO THE
ENGLISH EDITION

THE Norwegian edition of my book on Albert Schweitzer
aroused a lively discussion in the newspapers and in most
of our serious periodicals. From this it transpired that,
despite all that has been written by and about the doctor
of Lambarene, there was a great deal of disagreement
about the essentials of his life-view as I presented them
after my studies and extensive correspondence with him.
Typically, several writers with a philosophical training
agreed that I had emphasized the essential and most
important aspects of Schweitzer's views on religion and
morality, but I was also strongly attacked, particularly
from the theological camp, which at the same time cari-
catured the central features of Schweitzer's philosophy.
Some critics of the book even took that opportunity to
attack Schweitzer himself. My discussion of whether or
not Schweitzer can be regarded as a 'Christian' led to a
very emotional debate. The question, of course, depends
on what meaning you attach to the word 'Christian'—a
thing that is discussed in some detail in the final chapter
of this book. But it was just on this point that opinions
proved to be *most* divergent, even in theological circles.
As a result, while some theologians regarded Schweitzer's
view of religion as pure *heresy*, others found his doctrine
entirely in accordance with the gospels. As a result of
this discussion, I have added to the text for the English
edition a number of more general comments and omitted
particulars of the ecclesiastical controversy in Norway
which presumably is of little interest outside that
country.

As is mentioned on page 14, Schweitzer indicated that he would prefer it if his letters were not quoted verbatim but the essentials communicated in general terms. When the Norwegian was already printed I received from Schweitzer's secretary an answer to a letter of mine dated January 29, 1958 in which I had given a detailed summary in English of all the chapters and a broad indication of what I had taken to be his views on God, prayer and other concepts. I mentioned that I had intended to quote various points from his letters that were necessary in order that there should be no doubt as to his views on these. In the letter from Lambarene dated March 30, 1958, his secretary, Miss Ali Silver, regretted that Dr. Schweitzer was unable to reply to my letter of January 29th personally as he had hurt his right hand, and she went on to say:

'Dr. Schweitzer read your letter, in which you write about your book: 'Albert Schweitzer, a characterological study', with great interest and he is convinced that the decisions are in good hands. Dr. Schweitzer asked me to tell you that you are free to do what you think right. Enclosed are two plans of the hospital, as I don't know which one you prefer to be printed on the inside of the book-cover.'

I have felt impelled to quote this letter,[1] as I have been accused from several quarters, especially the theological, of having misunderstood Schweitzer when I assert, for example, that he does not believe in the Christian God as a kind of personal God, and that on the whole he does not seek contact with any Divinity other than Being itself. In order further to substantiate that Schweitzer

[1] The quotation is here published with the special consent of Dr. Schweitzer as given in a letter dated Lambarene, July 28, 1959.

has found that on essential points my 'decisions are in good hands', I would like as introduction to this English edition to quote part of my letter to Schweitzer of January 29, 1958, in which I outlined my understanding of his philosophy as I presented it in my book. Here I wrote, among other things:

'As to your *conception of God,* I have described how you are of the opinion that "God" is a historical symbol which, because it is an abstraction, cannot have any real content. You are of the opinion that we can meet God only in *Being* and by acting out in love the will to live among other wills to live we fulfil the essential purpose of Life. As to *Prayer,* I have stated that you do not—as Christians usually do—direct this to a transcendental God. According to your opinion, Prayer is an act of meditation during which you seek contact with the primary eternal source which gives us the force to stay the difficulties of life and help us to fulfil our higher destiny.

'As to *the Figure of Jesus,* I have made a little summary of your book: *Die Psychiatrische Studie von Jesus,* and I have also stated that you do not consider Jesus as a real son of God but you consider him as the greatest ethical personality which has ever lived. As is the case with all great personalities to which we are emotionally related, Jesus has a mystical power to influence our ethical Life. In the following chapters I point to the great significance of honesty in thinking also in questions of religion and morals, which you stress. I have made a special attempt to explain how you are the first Thinker in the West who does not stop thinking at the border of the irrational world, and I state that I fully agree with you that all thinking must end in the irrational. In fact it is among other things the only standpoint a scientist can take.

'In the last chapter I cite your discussion of the different religious systems and come to the conclusion that in fact you do not belong to any of them.'

When Schweitzer had his secretary write that he is '*convinced* that the decisions are in good hands', I feel that I can be sure of having correctly understood the essentials of his views on the concepts mentioned.

The main purpose of this book has never been to incite controversy as to how far Schweitzer can be regarded as being a Christian. From my point of view that is a purely theoretical question which the theologians must decide. My purpose has been to help to make clear where Schweitzer stands with regard to the central questions in any philosophy of life of religious character, and also to throw light on his rich and ethically valuable personality from my knowledge of his work and the fundamental traits of his character. My personal correspondence with him has made me feel specially eager to oppose the tendency of some writers to reduce the value of Schweitzer's achievements to the commonplace and to interpret his personality in a way that to my mind reveals a complete lack of ability to comprehend the basic motives of his work.

G. LANGFELDT

Oslo, May 1959

I

THE ESSENTIAL TRAITS
OF ALBERT SCHWEITZER'S
PERSONALITY

WHEN attempting to investigate the characteristics of some outstanding personality, one will usually find that these have been evident since childhood and early youth. It is, however, seldom that there are thoroughly reliable sources of information about this person's early life. What parents and brothers and sisters have to tell is often strongly coloured by the emotional fixation that is usually found to be present, while the impressions of those who are not so closely related and of mere acquaintances tend to be more superficial and may not even be concerned with the essential traits. A very thorough knowledge of the person concerned, acquired through real intimacy presupposing great frankness on either side, is required in order to be able to understand the fundamental attributes of a personality. Often, however, outstanding personalities are reserved and perhaps even rather shy. They have opened their hearts to a single friend, perhaps, but such friends of the great seldom write their biographies. One source of analysis are biographical works based on studies of what literary works the subject may have written. Such analyses often produce valuable data, even though that may be capable of several different interpretations. An autobiography is undoubtedly a good source of knowledge about a great figure, though it may have its weaknesses. For example, the author may be no great hand at discerning and describing his own qualities. There are a number of other pitfalls for those trying to discover an author's basic qualities from what he has written of himself: his autobiography may have had a certain purpose other than that of just describing himself and his experiences. Even such pure description may be tendentious, the author showing himself in a more flattering light than objectively he deserves, while his associates have unreal motives attributed to them for motives of which the author may or may not be conscious. Thus the worth of an autobiography depends very much on the author's realism, integrity, emotional balance and freedom from complexes that could more or less subconsciously affect a description that the author might have intended to be utterly objective.

Where Albert Schweitzer is concerned we are in the happy position of having a very simple, but most charming little autobiography, *Memoirs of Childhood and Youth*. It appears to have no pretension to be other than a description of a number of the experiences Schweitzer had from his earliest childhood until he left school. It begins with a description of the little town of Kaysersberg in Upper Alsace where Schweitzer was born on January 14, 1875, and it ends with the thoughts that occupied him in 1893 while he was preparing for his final examination before leaving school. Many big books have been written about Albert Schweitzer, his personality and his work. They have all had to use this little book as their source for understanding the essentials of the gigantic ethical personality that Schweitzer is. In my opinion there is no reason to analyse the information the reader gets in this autobiography before evaluating it. Being the courageous seeker after truth that he is, and with his absolute integrity, we can safely assume that the descriptions of his experiences and his own reflections on them are as sober and correct as one could wish. The book was first published in 1924 when Schweitzer was forty-nine, so we may presume that his memory was good and not in any way an obstacle to reproducing his material. The usual psychological considerations would make it an inviting task to undertake a more detailed analysis of, e.g., the way in which he strongly emphasizes that it was always consideration for others (his schoolfellows, teacher of singing, the cripple) that called forth his immediate reactions to his own behaviour to them. We know, for instance, that *wanting to be like the others* can be a symptom of weakness indicating little strength of will and a dependence upon others. In our schools it calls for no little strength of character not to copy the others where dress, make-up, amusements, sexual morality, etc., are concerned. We accept the fact that it was always consideration for others that was the motive for his actions, but this can be, of course, because we have no knowledge of other motives, conscious or unconscious, that might indicate the contrary. There have, in fact, been one or two critics who have thought they have found traits in Schweitzer that they consider far from likeable. Thus, Professor P. G. Lindhardt, a well-known Danish theologian, published in *Jyllandsposten* of October 5, 1958, a description of Albert Schweitzer the effect of which could be quite crushing. 'Like the pelican in one of his own books, he likes to be photographed in interesting attitudes,' he wrote. 'His ethical reactions are skilfully used to depict his own greatness.' And again: 'His ethical self-perfection is quite simply a subtle and self-indulgent form of self-righteousness.' According to Professor Lindhardt, Schweitzer has done 'a good job of work, but no better than any artisan or housewife who, loyal and unnoticed, gets on with the job'. And again: ' "Reverence for Life" has aroused much enthusiasm because it can mean anything and everything.' Lindhardt's peculiar attitude to Schweitzer's life's work fortunately is exceptional in the North and throws more light on the Professor himself, than on Schweitzer. At all events, it demonstrates a striking lack of ability—or will—to appreciate the essentials of Schweitzer's personality. Where Schweitzer is concerned, however, it never for a moment occurs to me to attribute to him other motives than those he himself adduces, because we know him through his work and have seen that this has arisen out of just those characteristics that he describes in his autobiography. Schweitzer himself has written that he thinks people ought to be careful about analysing each other's mental properties except for very special purposes that can be to the advantage of the person concerned. We will take note of that here for our appraisal of him based on his own writings. We accept at once that what he writes about himself is the best source of information we can have for understanding his personality. He is entitled to that declaration of confidence. And so in this book I shall abstain from any depth-psychological appraisal of certain features of his personality. It is true that Schweitzer himself has not always abstained from analysing other people's mental components. In *The Psychiatric Study of Jesus*, for example, he has subjected the various sides of Jesus' personality to a thorough examination. But this had the specific purpose of demonstrating that Jesus was not mentally deranged as has been maintained in a number of psychiatric studies.

Besides in depth-psychological studies of personalities based on their writings one has to be very wary of drawing definite conclusions.

One can, no doubt, postulate that individual personalities described are mouthpieces for the author or one can hold that there is identification with one or several of these persons. But unless one is personally acquainted with the author and knows his intentions in writing his book, there is no doubt that it is easy to get on to the wrong track. Therefore, in what follows I shall confine myself to what Schweitzer has written about himself, though occasionally I may make use of information taken from authors who were personally acquainted with Albert Schweitzer.

*

According to Schweitzer's autobiographical writings there would seem to be two powerful traits in his personality that have brought him to the position that he has now occupied for over a generation.

First and foremost there is his *strong sympathy* for *all* his fellow-creatures. When still a schoolboy he was greatly perturbed when occasionally he witnessed some act of thoughtlessness towards an animal, such as he describes in *Memoirs of Childhood and Youth*:

'As far back as I can remember, I was saddened by the amount of misery I saw in the world around me. Youth's unqualified *joie de vivre* I never really knew, and I believe that to be the case with many children, even though they appear outwardly merry and quite free from care.

'One thing that specially saddened me was that the unfortunate animals had to suffer so much pain and misery. The sight of an old limping horse tugged forward by one man while another kept beating it with a stick to get it to the knacker's yard at Colmar, haunted me for weeks.'

One will seldom find a better description of entirely *direct* sympathy with animals and it shows us how that seemingly completely spontaneous expression of his philosophy, 'Reverence for Life', that came to him in Lambarene, in reality was the result of a disposition that we must regard as congenital. He has also written: 'The greatest experience of my childhood and youth was when the commandment that we shall not kill or torture came to life within me. All else pales beside that.' The most charming expression of his love for and *identification* with our animal fellows in my opinion is to be found in his little book *A Pelican Tells of Its Life.* Here he identifies himself entirely with the pelican which tells of its experiences in Lambarene, and projects into the pelican's mental processes his own sympathy with all living creatures, his own suffering when others are thoughtless towards them and his gratitude when he sees that an apparently evil action had no evil intent. The book starts with these lines: 'I am the pelican that you will find so many pictures of in this book, and now I want to tell you who I am and some of the things that I have experienced.' When the 'Doctor Miss' indicated that she regarded the pelican as an interesting model and said to another white person: 'It (the pelican) loves being photographed in interesting attitudes, so it sits quite still, the vain creature,' the pelican is made to say: 'That remark wounded me deeply.' This little book gives us a vivid impression of how genuine and deeply felt, one can almost say rooted in religion, is Schweitzer's reverence for all that lives. But Schweitzer's descriptions of his own experiences with animals at the same time illustrate the fact that people—even the ethically most estimable—have tendencies to be both good and evil. An example of this is his story about his little dog Phylax: 'Like so many dogs it could not bear uniforms and always flew at the postman. Therefore it became my job to keep Phylax at a distance when the postman came. Phylax was not good-tempered and had even gone for a policeman. I used to drive it into a corner with a whip and only let it out when the postman had gone. It was a proud feeling to stand like a wild animal-tamer over the dog while it barked and bared its teeth, curbing it with a tap of the whip when it tried to escape. But that proud feeling did not last long. Later, when we were sitting side by side as good friends, I would reproach myself for having struck it. I knew that I could also have kept it from the postman if I had held it by the collar and patted it. But when the fateful moment came once more, I again yielded to the intoxication it afforded me to be the wild animal-tamer . . . ' What impressive self-knowledge that little story reveals! It seems to say: 'I acted wickedly although I had the possibility of achieving exactly the same result by employing love instead.'

Psychologically interesting, too, is his story about the chestnut horse that could not trot very far. Schweitzer, however, became intoxicated with the feel of the reins and gave way to the temptation of whipping it into a trot, even when he knew that it was tired. But then the reaction came almost immediately: 'But what became of my pleasure when we got home and I unharnessed it and noticed what I could not see so well from the trap, how the creature's flanks were labouring. What good was it then looking into its tired eyes and making a word-less appeal for forgiveness?' What an insight this simple, frank confession gives us into the ethical greatness of that human soul and especially into the complete spontaneity of the ethical reactions! We shall see that he showed all these ethical reactions so early in his child-hood that they could not have been the result of direct instruction or punishment. They were entirely spontaneous reactions which we must therefore regard as having been part of his inherent disposition. This does not apply only to his reactions to animals and his companions; he describes having had similar ethical reactions where his music teacher and other slighter acquaintances were concerned. As far as his school-fellows went, it was the principle of *reciprocity*—also an important side of his ethical disposition—that was particularly in evidence. He put himself so thoroughly in their place that he could see how they regarded him as 'the clergyman's son who had broth twice every single week'. That was what was thrown in his teeth one day when on the way home he wrestled with a boy who was supposed to be stronger than he and managed to throw him. 'As he lay there under me, he stammered out: "If I got broth twice every single week as you do, I'd be as strong as you." I went home, appalled at the way the tussle had ended. Georg Nitschelm had with bitter dis-tinctness put into words what I had often been made to feel: the boys in the village did not regard me as being altogether one of them. To them I was one who was better off, the clergyman's son, the son of a gentleman. I suffered because of that and wished that I was not better off than they. I took a loathing to broth.' And at once he did the logical thing: he refused to wear a smart sailor's cap, he wanted a cap like the village boys wore and he refused to walk in the street 'dressed as a gentleman'.

Not even a box on the ears and being locked in the cellar could make him alter his decision—even though he hated to disobey his parents. These forces that were brewing in young Albert Schweitzer must have been very powerful. Obviously, his attitude here was in no way due to cowardice or vanity. Where schoolchildren are concerned, the usual reaction is the opposite of Schweitzer's. They do not want to be like those who are *worst* off; no, what all children want is as many optimal advantages as the others: equally *smart* clothes, the same number of entertainments, equally great freedom. The decisive factors where Schweitzer was concerned were the principle of *solidarity* and his ability *to put himself in his companions' place*. It is true that his account of the incident shows that his sensitiveness was a strongly contributory factor. He often refers to this susceptibility in himself. We know, however, that this hypersensitiveness and squeamishness can express itself in many different ways. It can result in arrogance, in an attitude of bitter enmity, in over-compensation and many other attitudes that are not looked upon as particularly attractive. The proof of Schweitzer's greatness here is that all those other reactions were not present. Instead, he was dominated by a sense of solidarity with his schoolmates showing that he had been able to put himself utterly in their place.

27

Charming, too, is his description of how he reacted when he suddenly discovered that he was better than his singing teacher who could only play the music of the psalm with one finger, while he sat down and played straight off with harmonies.

'In my eagerness I sat down at the harmonium and played the melody with harmonies straight off. At that she became very friendly and gave me a strange look. But she continued to play the chorale with one finger. Then I realized that I could do something that she could not, and I felt ashamed of having shown her my skill which I had taken quite as a matter of course.'

What a lot we have to learn from Schweitzer and just from these thoughts of his boyhood! Aren't most of us often eager to demonstrate how much cleverer we are than everyone else—and what fools others can be? And we do so even though we may discover, when thinking it over, that our superiority is due to certain advantages that we have been given quite undeservedly, while those on whom we have exercised our superiority are not so favourably placed.

I have devoted so much attention to Schweitzer's early ethical reactions because I consider that they are fundamental for understanding his work and personality. But there is another, special side to his reactions which I must point out here: namely, that his ethical reactions to his own bad behaviour were always so *immediate*. As has already been stated, they were not the result of direct reproach or punishment; they came immediately, almost as a consequence of the bad action itself. There are few descriptions of such reactions that can better show how *good* is implanted in people in the same way as evil, and it is also an illustration of how, when an ethical disposition is sufficiently well developed, the good often triumphs without there being any need for reference to a moral code. It is true that Schweitzer grew up in a good, sheltered home and had a father who was an easy-going priest and taught him the Christian ethic and tolerance. There is no doubt that this up-bringing, probably through identification with his father, did much to initiate and promote his ethical development. But the ethical reactions he describes cannot be attributed to specific instruction and it is evident that these are independent, autonomous, ethical reactions. After his childhood it was the person of Jesus and His ethic that exerted the dominating influence on Albert Schweitzer and stimulated him to strive to live according to his doctrine. But, as we shall see later, Schweitzer himself was fully aware that good is im-planted in people and that it is not the case, that we should never have got the idea of a morally perfect world if we had not obtained it from Jesus—'It is natural to us and grows out of moral will'. Schweitzer's auto-biography makes it possible to conclude that he was equipped by Nature with very special abilities for ethical development. His early manifestation of the most valuable ethical reactions is a definite argument in support of the contention that man has a capacity for good implanted in him and that this capacity will usually develop if the person's surroundings and upbringing are favourable. But, at the same time, Schweitzer's development shows that a person who wishes to develop in an ethically worthy direction must also work on his own development, analyse his own successful and unsuccessful reaction-tendencies and employ both will and understanding to promote good.

This brings us to another feature of Schweitzer's personality that is most prominent and must be said to have been equally decisive for his whole life-view and work. This is his *unconditional insistence on truth and objective thinking*. This requirement has been predominant in his attitude to the traditional truths. He has shown, especially in his big works on research into the life of Jesus and on the apostle Paul, how he found support for this requirement of absolute truth in the words of the apostle Paul. We shall come back to this later, because it is so decisive for Schweitzer's attitude to the philosophy of life and the basis of morality, but I mention it here already, because it is quite clear from his book *Memoirs of Childhood and Youth* that he very early realized the importance of thinking. It looks as though his need of independent intellectual acceptance of the content of his faith made itself felt with the same compulsion and spontaneity as his ethical reactions. He was already thinking for himself when old Pastor Wennagel was preparing him for confirmation. He writes: 'I realized that on one point I thought differently from the way he did, despite all my respect for him. He wanted to make us see that where faith was concerned, thought must be silent. But I was, and remain, convinced that the truth in Christianity should be proved through thinking. I told myself that we have been given minds in order that we should be able to comprehend even the loftiest thoughts of religion. The certainty of this filled me with joy.' Further on, he describes how his reaction against all stereotyped thinking resulted in his having a rather awkward period from his fourteenth to his sixteenth year. 'I had such an urge to discuss things that I became quite intolerable to other people, especially to

Father. I wanted to discuss every question that cropped up in any connection with the utmost earnestness and strict logic. I wanted to unmask all the mistakes of routine thinking and drag out into the light what was correct. The pleasures of searching for the truth took hold of me like an intoxication.' As we know, this innate urge to seek out the truth resulted in his having to make a definite break with the whole of Christian dogma and there is reason to believe that when he took that step, he had a certain feeling of intoxication too, even though aware of the disquiet he knew his action must occasion among Christians. One can safely assume that, when he describes so well the sense of liberation the negro convert feels on being freed from his belief in fetishes, it is because he has a sympathetic insight into the negro's emotions. Schweitzer had certainly experienced the same feeling of liberation.

Schweitzer's tremendous urge to understand existence and its meaning inevitably meant that he felt impelled to enrich his mind by *reading*. Of this he writes: 'My craving for reading was limitless. I still have it. I am quite unable to put down a book I have begun. I would rather read all night. At the very least I must have skimmed through it to the very end. If I like it, I may well read it through two or three times in succession. My aunt thought that this "gluttony" for books, as she called it, was the real cause . . . '

Though Schweitzer very early accepted the idea that the truth of Christianity must be demonstrated by thinking, he did not allow his thinking to reject the existence of the great unknown. In his description of science teaching at his school, he expatiates on how little we really understand of what goes on in Nature: 'I really hated the science text books. Their confident explanations, intended to be learned by heart, did not in any way satisfy me—apart from the fact that I quickly discovered that they were rather out-of-date. I thought it ridiculous that there should be explanations of the wind, rain, snow, hail, of the origin of clouds, spontaneous ignition of hay, Trade Winds, the Gulf Stream, thunder and lightning. I had always thought it especially puzzling how rain-drops, snowflakes and hail were made. It offended me that the absolute mysteriousness of Nature was not recognized, that they spoke confidently of explaining, when in reality all they had done was to provide a more detailed description that only made the mystery more mysterious still. I realized then that what we describe as force and "life" by its real nature will always remain inexplicable.' This quotation really gives us the key to understanding both Schweitzer's world-view and his life-view with ethical mysticism as its emotional component. This reverential, humble attitude to the unknown in Nature gradually came to dominate his attitude to the laws—or lack of laws and logic—that appear to govern nature. And later he declared himself to be a definite *agnostic* as far as world-view was concerned; but where life-view was concerned, the meaning of life and his attitude to the unknown, he declared himself an *ethical mystic*. This latter means, what we shall be discussing later, that he believes there to be implanted in all people a *will-to-live* that is linked with the primal force, God—'or whatever one likes to call it', as he writes—But this ethical mysticism bears no relation to ordinary mysticism that sets the unknown as a force *outside* the person. He definitely repudiates the absolute as an abstraction, since such an abstraction only results in the use of words or symbols that cannot be visualized and therefore have no reality in themselves.

There are other traits in Schweitzer's personality that we can discover by reading his little autobiography. His *strength of will* showed itself very early, e.g. when he insisted on that act of solidarity with his schoolmates over dress that has been described earlier. Otherwise it is enough to say that before he was thirty-eight he had taken degrees in three disciplines—philosophy, theology and medicine. That itself is a unique feat that not only proves how all-round his talents are, and what a wealth of interests he has, but is evidence of the possession of most impressive energy and will-power. There is no doubt that Schweitzer very early understood the necessity of deliberately employing his will-power to encourage the good side of his character. Of this latter he writes in his autobiography that he learned the importance of it from his schoolmaster, Dr. Wehrmann: 'From him I learned that a deep sense of duty is the great educative force. It will do what no admonishment or punishment will accomplish.' And of course, when speaking of Schweitzer's aptitudes, one has to mention his *musical talent*. Countless articles have been written about it, and here I shall only just say that obviously his musical talent must be viewed in close connection with his religious and ethical-mystical gifts. Common to both is the ability to make oneself one with the mysterious which gives people experiences that are difficult to describe in words and still more difficult to explain. It is these experiences that ought to compel people to feel the profoundest respect for the unknown, even though not everyone has the ability to experience it. History has numerous convincing examples to show that these mystical sources often inspire the most worthy achievements even in practical works of charity.

Schweitzer's autobiography may perhaps dwell mainly on the positive traits in his personality, yet he has—no doubt with considerable effort—frankly and honestly described certain traits that are very human, but not usually regarded as creditable. It should be mentioned here that Schweitzer's attitude to this question of opening one's heart to other people is somewhat unusual and individual. He considers that even with those who are very close to one there should be the *some things* that are kept sacred and not revealed: 'We must accept the fact that we are a mystery to each other. To know one another does not mean knowing everything about each other. A person must not force his way into another's being. It is indelicate to analyse other people—except in cases where one is trying to help the mentally deranged. There is an intellectual as well as a physical modesty that we ought to respect. The mind, too, has its veil and that should not be torn away. None of us can say to another: since we belong together, I have a right to know all your thoughts. Not even a mother can be allowed to behave like that to her children. All such demands are stupid and unhealthy. Here it is just a question of saying: "Give the one with whom you walk together on your way as much of your intellectual life as you can, and receive as a precious gift what comes back to you from that one".'

Admittedly Schweitzer's attitude to the question of frankness between people would seem to be prompted by a delicate ethical intuition, but he does not appear to have realized that there is also a mental hygiene side to the question. It is naturally quite correct that one has no right uninvited to analyse the inmost feelings and thoughts of one's fellow beings. Everyone has a sovereign right to keep to himself as much of his mental life as he wishes. But one should remember that many who are shy by nature and have difficulty in making contacts will often be grateful for a gentle invitation to confide. It is not mentally healthy to keep conflicts and gloomy thoughts to oneself. And many people will not agree with Schweitzer where confidences between mother and daughter, for example, are concerned. An early established frankness between parents and children can be a great help throughout adolescence. But what parents can learn from Schweitzer is that they have no *right* to intrude upon their children's mental life. What sins are not committed against this ethical commandment, for example, when children reach the age of puberty and quite naturally wish to have certain secrets. 'Reverence for life' also includes reverence for other people's lives and thoughts. It may sound strange that a psychiatrist whose business it is to get to the bottom of the mental processes of the sick as far as he can, is able so wholeheartedly to subscribe to this idea; but the psychiatrist only acts on invitation from those concerned, or when a patient needs help, yet is not himself aware of his aberration, and in this case even Schweitzer considers it permissible to break that commandment. But where the healthy are concerned, the rule must be that it must always be the *other* party who *wants to be helped*. Schweitzer does realize, however, that there can be danger in being too reserved with people. What he especially stresses is considerateness, tact. In this connection he writes: 'Naturally we must take care to be tactful with each other and not meddle with other people's concerns gratuitously. But we must also be aware of the danger of such reserve. It is wrong to let oneself be compelled to be an absolute stranger to another person. People belong together, man has a right to man. Conditions can occur that cause distance to be abolished. The law of reticence is fated to be broken by the rights of the heart.'

The fact that Schweitzer's autobiography contains no real confidential information of significance for understanding certain sides of his personality must be seen against this background of his attitude to the question of frankness with one's fellow beings. It is foreign to his nature to inform the public of the more intimate details of his development. This fits in with his whole ethical personality, which tells him that certain aspects of a person's life are the private property of the individual and not suitable for publication. A little more of this ethical modesty would not be out of place, for example, in the literary world. Those who defend the tendency of novels to describe, *inter alia*, people's sexual life in detail, as though it were a species of animal life without spiritual components, ought to take note of Schweitzer's view of intellectual modesty. At all events, certain spheres of association of the two sexes ought to be accorded greater respect than is shown today, when they are exposed publicly for the lust of those who need that sort of substitute.

Another reason for Schweitzer's advocacy of reticence must be his *reserve*. Of this he writes: 'I inherited my reserve from Mother. We lacked the ability to express the love we felt for each other in words. I could count the number of times we had a real heart to heart talk. But we understood each other without talk.' Nor have talk or philosophizing been characteristic of Schweitzer since. He has *acted* and let his actions speak for themselves. Of this we can say that we understand him without a more explicit explanation being necessary. Nor does Schweitzer in any way disguise the fact that his was a *choleric temperament.* 'From my mother I also got a passionate temper, which she got from her father, who was both kindhearted and hot-tempered. It was while playing that I first realized this side of my nature. I took every game in deadly earnest and became angry if the others failed to enter into it heart and soul . . . I have had to fight very hard against this hot temper. I am aware of many events of my childhood that humiliate me and keep me alert in this struggle.' In this connection we ought to mention a trait from his earliest childhood which points to *sensation-seeking and the desire to attract attention.* He writes in his autobiography: 'Another memory from my very early childhood is that of the occasion when I first consciously felt ashamed.' He had been stung by a bee while his father was removing honey from their hives. 'The entire household came running because of my screams,' he writes, 'and everyone was sorry for me. Mother reproached Father for starting to remove the honey without first seeing that I was beyond the reach of danger. This made me very interesting . . . My conscience told me that I ought to stop now. But to make myself more interesting I went on bawling and accepted comfort that I did not need. In reality I thought that I had behaved badly and I was unhappy because of it for days. How often, as an adult, has this experience been a warning and saved me from the temptation of making a fuss when something upset me.'

37

One must admire Schweitzer for his ability to analyse his own tendencies in his very early childhood, but at the same time one cannot help noticing how differently he reacted to others of that age. Most children would have considered it perfectly right and proper to receive commiseration in a similar situation, and many no doubt without analysing their motives, would accentuate a propensity (in this case to bawl) that could bring more self-satisfaction. But Schweitzer learns how to use even this experience for his experiments in ethical self-perfection, which, along with altruism, he considers to be the corner-stone of all ethics. Many children who develop this tendency to sensationalism and wanting to be the centre of attention early and then acquire a taste for it, often develop into real hysterics and, when grown-up, can have an immoderate urge to cause a stir and will often have recourse to dramatic devices in order to experience the pleasures of doing so. Schweitzer's anecdote teaches us that this can be avoided by self-discipline in one's early years and parents should remember that, for there are not many children who, like Schweitzer, can educate themselves at such an early stage.

It is obvious that from his earliest childhood Schweitzer worked to educate himself to behave in a morally worthy manner. An example of this is when he let himself be inveigled by the other boys into joining them in teasing the Jew Mausche. 'But Mausche walked on with his freckles and his beard, as calm as the donkey. Only once in a while did he turn and give us an embarrassed, but good-natured smile. That smile overwhelmed me. Mausche was the first to teach me what it meant to be able to keep silent under persecution. He became very important for my education.' 'It was and always has been this Mausche with his forgiving smile who compels me to be patient when I am tempted to fume and storm.' This is a temptation to which Schweitzer must often have been subjected, but he has always practised the art of following the example of the Jew, Mausche. In a shameful attack on Schweitzer made in the monthly organ of the Scottish Church (the issue of September 3, 1957), Rev. Dr. Finlayson said that while Schweitzer has been hailed as the world's greatest medical missionary, musician, philosopher and 'I don't know what', those who had visited his hospital at Lambarene had a different tale to tell. According to their accounts nothing was ever killed in the hospital precincts and that applied to insects and animals that deposited their droppings everywhere, even on the operating table; while animals with serious infections mingled with the white staff and the patients. Schweitzer, the writer went on to say, was rightly regarded as being more a Buddhist than a Christian, and all those facts, unpleasant though they were, only went to show that if a person gave up the New Testamentary conception of Christianity, he also gave up all the principles of Christianity and all trace of Christian activities.

In my correspondence with Schweitzer I mentioned this attack, which had been reported even in Norwegian papers, and asked him if he could ever be bothered to contradict that sort of thing. His reply showed that he was still practising what he had learned from Mausche. He wrote that he had long since ceased to correct false-hoods about him published in the Press. And he was not particularly concerned that theologians took offence at his ideas.

It was Schweitzer's humility and also his sense of gratitude and its connected urge to make some sacrifice for others, that really lay behind his decision to go to Africa to help primitive peoples. This sense of gratitude was another thing that made itself felt early in his childhood, as he himself relates in his autobiography: 'It became more and more apparent to me that I had no right to take my happy youth, my health and power to work for granted. Out of this, my very profound sense of happiness, there gradually grew understanding of Jesus' saying that we cannot keep our lives for ourselves. Those who have had much from life, must give correspondingly much in return. Those who have been spared suffering are called upon to feel, help and mitigate the suffering of others. We must all join in bearing the burden of misery that lies upon the world. This idea worked in me, muddled and far from clear. On many occasions it let go of me for a while and I felt relieved and thought that I could be master of my life once more. But a little cloud had appeared on the horizon. At times I was able to disregard it, but it grew slowly and continually, and in the end it covered the whole sky.

'My decision was made when I was twenty-one. I was at home from the university for the Whitsun holiday, and I decided then that I would live for preaching, science and music till I was thirty. If, by that time, I had accomplished in science and art what I had set myself to do, I would take up direct service for humanity. What form this would take, I imagined would be shown me by circumstances in the meantime.

'The resolve to devote myself to medical work in the colonies did not come till later. It came to me after I had had several plans for other kinds of help and had given

them up again for various reasons. A chain of circumstances then showed me the way to those suffering from
sleeping-sickness and leprosy in Africa.'

Later on, he describes in greater detail particular
things for which he is grateful: 'One thing moves me
when I think back to my youth: the fact that so many
people gave me something or were something to me
without themselves realizing it. People with whom I had
never exchanged a word, indeed some of whom I
had merely heard, have exerted a decisive influence on
me.' And 'We have to thank others for much of the
goodness, strength to forgive, truthfulness, faithfulness,
patience in suffering that there is in our lives.' Here we
encounter a gospel that all can benefit from listening to.
Do not most of those who are well situated economically
and spiritually take that almost as a matter of course?
How many express their gratitude to others for being
able to wake in health each day and be let off with far
fewer worries than many others? Does it occur to any
of us that we *have no right* to accept so much good
without giving something in return? If the spirit of
Schweitzer could enter into people in this respect we
would not be *far* from having the kingdom of God on
Earth.

*

The above quotations give a vivid impression of how
the various traits of Schweitzer's personality have
developed with almost compulsive consistency, like a
natural law that led inevitably to the development of
one of the greatest ethical personalities of our time.
Schweitzer himself had a feeling that the trend of his
development was laid down when he was still very

young, and that the qualities he exhibited then were the lasting, valuable ones. The last section of his little autobiography begins with the following sentences:

'The ideas which determine our character and life are implanted in mysterious fashion. When we are leaving childhood behind us, they begin to shoot up. When we are seized by youth's enthusiasm for the good and the true, they burst into flower and the fruit begins to set. In the development which follows the one really important thing is—how much still remains of the fruit, the buds of which were put out in its spring-time by the tree of our life.'

The following chapters with the light they will throw on the attitude Schweitzer came to take towards the Christian religion and the basis of morality will convince us that this is true in every respect, at any rate where Schweitzer is concerned. We shall show how his *courage*, his *uncompromising search for the truth* and his insistence on *rational thinking* early led to his breaking with Christian dogma. His *strength of will* made it possible for him to realize the plan he made at the age of twenty-one for completing his theological, medical and musical studies before he was thirty and to carry out his plan of sacrificing himself for humanity. But, all the time, the *driving force* within him has been the mighty ethical predisposition which, through his compassion with all living creatures, his sense of being duty-bound to do something in return for the good he had himself received and his great sense of responsibility, impelled him to carry through the resolve that he obviously considered to have been implanted in him by the great mysterious primal force. So far, Schweitzer's achievement is clear and easily comprehensible in ordinary psychological analysis. But one will not have understood his personality aright if one does not grant equal weight to the more mystical forces working in him. One can safely say that Schweitzer's is a deeply religious nature, even though his rationalism has prevented him rooting his religion and ethics in the transcendental. The difference between his conception of the mysterious primal force as an 'ethical God-personality' and the ordinary abstract God-symbols would appear to be merely one of degree; yet even so his rejection of a *'human* God-personality' (which is the term for the Christians' God used in a letter to me) is of the greatest consequence for his attitude to incarnation, the sacraments and dogma, among other things. This really is an aspect of Schweitzer's personality that presents quite a little philosophical problem and is one with which several writers have concerned themselves. There is no doubt that his most important and most inspiring model has been Jesus Christ, and none either that as far as he has been able, he has tried to practise the ethics particularly of the Sermon on the Mount. One incentive here has been his humility and his feeling of gratitude towards those people who helped to make his childhood and youth relatively happy. He will therefore remain for all time as the personified ethical giant, a forerunner of the type of person who, we must hope, can come about if people will follow his call and try to carry the 'kingdom of God' into practice here on earth.

*

When you study Schweitzer's own writings, you get the strong impression that certain conflicting forces have been at work within him right from his childhood and that these have resulted, amongst other things, in a dualistic attitude to the concept of God. It is obvious that it has been his marked rationalism—his insistence to himself that he is not going to accept anything but what his reason tells him, that has prevented him becoming a pure mystic. His need of mystical experience, however, is strongly expressed in his belief in a mystical primal force and this again has inspired his motto 'reverence for life'. Where his view of Jesus is concerned, it is obvious that he is fascinated by him, to such an extent that there are certain signs of identification. This has found expression, for example, in his urge to sacrifice himself for the black peoples and thereby expiate the sins of the white man. But his *reason* prevents him accepting the belief that Jesus is the son of God. But not even here can he free himself from the mystical link with Jesus. Oscar Kraus has called Schweitzer an *'Agnostiker im Nachfolge Kristi'* and seldom have four words contained so much of the essential. It will be my task in the following chapters to throw further light on Schweitzer's view of the concept of God and the Christian faith.

II

ALBERT SCHWEITZER'S VIEW
OF RELIGION AND ETHICS

The Concept of God

THAT Schweitzer is often regarded as a Christian is due
not least to the fact that in his writings he regularly
uses the term 'God' in the same sense as Christians do.
Both in his sermons in Lambarene and when writing to
Christian friends and connections, he uses the term more
or less as in normal Christian usage. We know from him
himself and from those who have visited Lambarene
that he regularly assembles his people there for *prayer*.
In his 'Letter to a Confirmand' he thus uses the expression 'God' in the ordinary orthodox Christian way
without comment. In this letter he writes, 'You are a
confirmand and have taken the decision to go through
life as one of God's children. May you always try
seriously to act in accordance with that decision.' This
letter was one of the things that led Bishop Schjelderup
of Norway to assume that Albert Schweitzer had a
'simple, personal Christian faith'. Others have thought
that Schweitzer's idea of God was that of the Old
Testament, while others again have advocated the view
which I have long maintained, namely that Schweitzer
has definitely abandoned belief in God as an *abstraction*
which, as such, implies an actual reality.

In his writings, Schweitzer has stated quite clearly that
the traditional Christian concept of God is a mere

45

abstraction and that therefore it cannot be said to imply any reality. He stressed this point of view in *Civilization and Ethics,* where he says, among other things: 'the essence of God, the Absolute, Soul of the Universe and similar expressions do not mean anything real, but something that is abstracted and which for that reason one cannot conceive. The only reality is Being which manifests itself in phenomena'. And later on he writes: 'How can thinking lead to such a meaningless result as to get people to enter into spiritual relationship with an unreal product of the intellect? By falling for two temptations, one *general* and one *special*. When thought is compelled to express itself in words, it accepts as its own the abstractions and symbols that are coupled with the actual language. This partnership, however, is only for the purpose of allowing us to present the matter in an abbreviated form, without having to propound it with all the details with which it was equipped. With time, however, thought comes to operate with these abstractions and symbols *as if* they represented something that really existed. This is the *general* temptation. The *special* temptation lies, in this case, in the fact that man's surrender to God is expressed through the use of abstractions and symbols in an attractively simple manner. This surrender is assumed to consist of a positive relation to Being as such, or to be more definite, the spiritual side of it. Intellectually, this sounds very attractive, but reality knows of no possibility for the individual to enter into a relationship with Being as such. As one in reality knows of no other form of Being than that manifesting itself in the existence of individuals so, too, one knows of no other relationships than those that one individual can have with another. Thus, if mysticism

46

is to be honest, the only thing it can do is to rid itself of the ordinary abstractions and admit that it cannot achieve anything rational with its imaginary concept of Being. To the honest mystic, *the absolute* is as meaningless as his fetish to the converted negro.' Further on, Schweitzer writes: 'It is only through the manifestations of Being and only through those with whom I enter into relationship, that I, as a being, have any relation to existence. My surrender to existence implies my surrender to all the manifestations of Being that require my surrender and to which I am in a position to surrender.'

In 1929, long before Schweitzer wrote this, Oscar Kraus[1] wrote that Schweitzer's theology was a strange mixture of agnosticism and animistic pantheism which Schweitzer himself has aptly called *ethical mysticism*.

In my opinion, the above quotations from Schweitzer not only give a relatively clear idea of his conception of God, but also provide the key to understanding his deeply religious surrender to all that lives. It must be quite clear from this exposition, which is *Schweitzer's own*, that he does not believe in the Christians' personal God and never addresses himself to God as an abstraction. He meets his God in identification with all that lives, animals, plants and people, and he holds that this is the only way in which one can meet God. In several of his books he has stated that we cannot apprehend and therefore cannot believe in any God *outside of* Being. For him God is the mysterious force that manifests itself in us as will-to-live. If we obey the call implanted in us, we will help to fulfil the purpose of life which is

[1] *Albert Schweitzer, sein Werk und seine Weltanschauung*, Berlin, 1929.

47

to promote 'the kingdom of God'. For Schweitzer, this latter is almost an ethical concept and to this we shall revert later. Thus, according to Schweitzer, both 'God' and 'the kingdom of God' are only to be found inside people themselves. Thus he writes in his *Philosophy of Civilization*: 'of inner necessity and without understanding the purpose of the world, I act upon the world by creating values and living ethically. For, through the world-genius and life-genius, I fulfil the universal will-to-live that manifests itself in me. I live my life in God, in the mysterious ethical God-personality that I do not apprehend in the world, but only experience as a mysterious will inside me.'

Schweitzer has obviously been strongly influenced by Spinoza who was outraged by the attempt made, out of consideration for the ethical world-view, to make God simultaneously an ethical personality *outside* the universe. If we compare what Schweitzer has written of God as an abstraction with his view of the will-to-live as a divine force manifesting itself in man, we can be left in no doubt about Schweitzer's conception of God.

It is quite true that in a letter, dated January 2, 1924, to Oscar Kraus, Schweitzer said that his conception of God lay somewhere between pantheism and theism. *'Um den Verzicht auf das Welterkennen komme ich nicht herum, über den Konflict Pantheismus-Theismus nicht hinaus. Dies sage ich sowohl in den philosophischen wie in der überlieferten theologischen Sprache,'* he wrote. Here, then, Schweitzer clearly declares himself an agnostic where world-view is concerned, while as regards the concept of God he admits to being in a conflict that confuses the concept for him—his conception of God lying somewhere between

pantheism and theism. It is surely not strange that even
Schweitzer can occasionally be in doubt when it comes
to purely philosophical explanation of the irrational. It
is possible, too, that he has gradually clarified his ideas.
Even though he can on occasion be somewhat ambiguous
in his attitude to the concept of God, he says again and
again in his writings that God cannot be apprehended
other than through this unknown force manifesting
itself in actual Being. It is presumably reasonable to
assume that Schweitzer has considerably altered his view
of the concept of God since he wrote that letter. He has
stuck to his agnosticism where world-view is concerned,
but as far as life-view goes, he has discovered that *life
has a meaning in itself* and that this lies in the will-to-
live which for him stands as the only manifestation of
the divine source. Because of that he disassociates
himself from any fusion with what he calls *pure God-
mysticism*.[1] 'God-mysticism, in the sense of a direct
becoming-one with the infinite creation will of God, is
impossible of realization. All attempts to extract living
religion from pure Monistic God-mysticism are fore-
doomed to failure . . . From the becoming-one with the
infinite essence of the being of the Universal Will-to-be
there can result nothing but a passive determination of
man's being, an absorption into God, a sinking into the
ocean of the Infinite. Pure God-mysticism remains a dead
thing.'

Thus, purely philosophically, it is, as has been said
already, quite clear that Schweitzer is an agnostic as far
as world-view is concerned, but an ethical mystic where
life-view is concerned.

Religion and ethics are related to each other in many
ways and we shall come back to this later. Here, when

[1] *The Mysticism of Paul the Apostle*, London, 1931.

discussing the concept of God, it will suffice to say that Schweitzer regards the world's lack of success in the sphere of ethics as being due not least to the fact that religious surrender is made to the abstract—to God. Thus he writes: 'But why, despite all efforts, has the ethic of self-perfection not become free of passivity? The reason is that it allows the spiritual, inner surrender to Being to be directed to an abstract notion of being instead of to actual being. Consequently it, too, falsely enters into nature-philosophy.' As far as becoming one with the great unknown, the absolute, goes, Schweitzer does not consider this either as ethical being. In the same paper he wrote: 'The experience of becoming one with the absolute, with the Being in the world-spirit, of fusing with God or whatever one likes to call it, is not in itself ethical, but intellectual.' One notices that here again Schweitzer uses the expression 'or whatever one likes to call it'. This itself is a sign that he has not been able to arrive at any concrete conception of the God to whom the Christians still address themselves in their prayers as though to a sort of 'human person'.

These quotations should have made it clear that Schweitzer considers it quite impossible to enter into any sort of *relationship* with an abstraction like God, since there cannot be any reality behind such an abstraction. But why is it, then, that he is continually using this expression as though it signified the Christians' God? The answer is simply this, that through the historical development that Schweitzer has pointed out, the name God has acquired the prescriptive right to represent the great unknown. Thus, if he wants to have any contact with Christians when discussing the 'origin of Being', he must use their expression.

But the *intention* of the term to Schweitzer is quite different from what it is to Christians, and this, too, he has explained so explicitly that no difference of opinion here should be possible. In his letter to Oscar Kraus, already mentioned, he said that he used the term God in two different ways. He wrote: 'So far, where philosophy is concerned, my principle has been to say no more than what was an absolutely logical experience of my thinking. Therefore in philosophy I never speak of "God" any more, but of the "universal will-to-live", of which I am conscious in two ways, namely as will-to-create outside me and as ethical will in me . . . On the other hand, if I am speaking the traditional language of religion, then I use the word "God" in its historical definition, in the same way as in ethics I say "love" instead of "reverence for life". My concern here is to give the thought experienced in its immediate lifelikeness and in its relation to traditional religiosity. That is why I make no concession either to nature philosophy or to religion. For both the intention remains entirely the same: Renunciation of understanding of the world and the establishment of priority for the universal will-to-live experienced in me.'

Schweitzer's purely philosophical view of the concept of God can be seen quite clearly from the following quotation.[1]

'Our relation to the primal origin of being that is manifest in us as the will-to-love is as to an ethical personality. Theism does not stand in opposition to pantheism, but rises out of it as the ethically definite of the indefinite.'

[1] From: *Albert Schweitzer. Denken und Tat.* Zusammengetragen und dargestellt von Rudolf Grabs. Reichard Meines Verlag in Hamburg, 1950.

Elsewhere, Schweitzer uses the expression 'the ethical god-personality' which also serves to emphasize that for him God is not an abstraction, but the concrete, even though unfathomable, will-to-live that, amongst other things, is manifested in love of all life. That makes his conception of God quite different to Jesus' conception of God which, of course, was the expression of a child-relationship to 'Our father which art in Heaven'. Accordingly, one must assume that, when he uses the expression 'God', Schweitzer generally employs it as the symbol of what Christian people on the whole believe in, though he himself, as a thinker and searcher after the truth, cannot work in terms of a personal God. It must be admitted, however, that to anyone not aware of this dual use of the concept of God, many of Schweitzer's writings must make it appear as though he held the ordinary Christian conception of God. This must be the reason why so many participants in the discussion in the Norwegian Press refused to accept the view of Schweitzer's conception of God that I published in 1956 in *Samtiden* and elsewhere.

In a letter to me of April 4, 1957, Schweitzer explained his conception of God in considerable detail and this agrees entirely with the quotation given above. In my letter to him I had stated what I took his conception of God to be and he wrote in his reply that I had put things just as they were and as he had experienced them. He mentioned in this letter that the first person to have taken up the problem of God along the same lines as he, was Spinoza in his *Deus sive Natura*, which had made a great impression on him as a student. In this letter he further elaborated his concept of God and said that our greater knowledge of nature and its essence takes us further on, beyond the idea of a God, analogous to a human being, who rules the world. We thereby lose the element of comfort there was in the old idea, but, on the other hand, our religion becomes purified and more clear. This results, among other things, in a tendency for *ethics* to become more and more the centre of religion. Ethics becomes the absolute that stands above religion. *Notions of faith* thus becomes relative and in reality it is this fact that characterizes this whole development. He goes on to say that the most important thing is to recognize that it is *the ethical* that decides our human nature and piety. And, he says further on, piety depends not on man being able to subscribe to a historically traditional conception of God, but on his being seized by the spirit and walking in it. And then comes something that emphasizes this point of why he still uses the concept of God and other religious notions.

The fact that he will still use the traditional language of religion, is due to the times and consideration for those who still think in terms of the historical traditional ethical religion. That Schweitzer still considers himself as belonging to Christendom is, according to his letter, because Christianity is the traditional ethical religion. The letter ends with a few lines utterly in keeping with his optimistic hope of the coming of the Kingdom of God on earth: 'But more and more will people be carried beyond the traditional ideas and experience piety as resulting from the spirit, as that which transcends all our ideas . . . '

If this prophecy is to be fully understood, I had better mention that in this letter he defines God thus: 'God is spirit, that is to say that which cannot be apprehended.' And he thinks that if the world will develop along these lines, then we shall gradually become aware of the *spiritual as such,* as it is continually being manifested in life on earth and its development and which will gradually become the power to which we submit in order to be at peace with ourselves. This agrees with all that Schweitzer has written elsewhere in showing that what is ordinarily called *God* is to him the mystical primal cause of being which reveals itself in us as the ethical power that conditions our efforts to do what is good and practise love. It must at all events be quite clear that Schweitzer does not believe in a personal God to whom one can turn for forgiveness of one's sins or from whom one can obtain other direct comfort. When he uses the concept God in ordinary Christian usage, as he frequently does, it is because he wishes to use the traditional language when writing and so meet those he is addressing on the level of their own religious notions. If one is to understand Schweitzer's conception of God, one must never lose sight of the fact, mentioned earlier, that it is not possible to enter into relation with the spirit that is usually called God except through surrender to 'real Being'. Here Schweitzer moves ethics and religion so close together as to make them indistinguishable. And if there is to be any question of one having to be absolute in relation to the other, then that one is *ethics.* Religion and all the dogma, ritual and practices that it is linked with becomes secondary in relation to the other.

Having thus arrived at Schweitzer's view of the concept of God, as that which represents the mysterious spirit or power which he considers to have real existence in actual Being, our next task must be to try and elucidate the origin and nature of this source of power. Before we start on this, however, there is one question

54

that obtrudes itself and requires an answer. I, like others, have found it difficult to understand that a person holding such a conception of God as we have described, could make such regular use of prayer as, according to all accounts from Lambarene, Schweitzer does. Schweitzer has written very little by way of explanation of what are his views on prayer, but all the same we shall examine this in the next chapter and try to throw some light upon it.

Prayer

Schweitzer, as we have said, has written very little about prayer and its significance. It is possible to conclude from his attitude to the concept of God and the roots of ethics that for him prayer is not an attempt to enter into contact with the great unknown, the absolute. He says forthright (in *Civilization and Ethics*) that abstraction means the death of both religion and ethics, and, knowing as we do from his own writings, that for him the great unknown only exists as the mysterious ethical primal force, it should go without saying that prayer to him cannot be an attempt to enter into contact with a personal divinity. The only place where I can find that Schweitzer has written anything at all direct about— vain—attempts to get into contact with the absolute, is in *Kultur und Ethik,* where he says: 'It is only an infinitesimal part of the infinite Being that comes within my scope. All the rest sails past me like ships far away, to which I send signals *without being understood.* (My italics.) But when I surrender to that which comes within my scope and which needs me, I put spiritual, inner surrender to infinite Being into practice and thereby give my wretched existence meaning and riches.'

After that, we must assume that to Schweitzer *prayer* means meditation and is a positive attempt to obliterate his conscious 'Ego' and thereby achieve greater solidarity with the primal cause of Being. He has said as much in a letter to me dated May 8, 1957, in which he writes that prayer means surrender to the spirit that is revealed in us in order that we can thereby achieve peace and the strength to bear all the burdens that are laid upon us.

Now, there are different views of prayer even within the theological world. There is one explanation of prayer which can be taken to represent the view of the Catholic Church and it would be interesting to consider it. In Bishop Jacob Manger's *Pastoral Letter for Lent* 1937,[1] he writes at one point: 'What does it mean to pray? To pray means to talk to God and with God, to lift up mind and heart to God or to collect oneself in Him, to associate with God either as a creature with his creator and a servant with his master or—and especially this—as a child with its father and a friend with his friend. We can never lose sight of the fact that God is our creator and master and that one day He will be our judge. Even so, prayer is first and foremost a talk with God as our father and our friend.'

We see how radically different this view of prayer is from Schweitzer's. There can be no doubt that Schweitzer has been very considerably influenced by the religious nature-philosophy of the oriental religions (Brahmanism, Buddhism, Laotse, Tsungtse, Hinduism). In particular the way in which these religions regard fusion with and loving surrender to God as the essential is strongly reminiscent of Schweitzer's view of prayer.

[1] *St. Olav.* Catholic Magazine for Religion and Culture, 1937. Oslo, Norway.

Probably his conception of God has also been influenced by both Brahmanism and Buddhism, for which God is not a person, but—as Schweitzer writes in his book on these religions — 'the pure, impersonal, spiritual principle'.

From this it is evident that for Schweitzer prayer is the attempt to identify himself with the primal cause of being, the nature of which he cannot, however, apprehend. A necessary consequence of this must be that Schweitzer never addresses himself directly to 'God' in the form of prayer. He does not believe that 'God' hears prayers he thinks that the signals that people send in that direction miss their mark. In none of Schweitzer's works have I found recorded any prayer that he has prayed, and I take it that he never recites the Lord's Prayer as a personal prayer to a supernatural instance. How different from our clergy who in their preaching are continually addressing monologues to God as though he were a human person and listened to them—and even answered! But even though Schweitzer is thus unable to abstract the deity and address himself to it in prayer, surrender to the mysterious primal force is none the less to him a source of constant renewal and a help in bearing the burdens of the day. That Schweitzer holds views different from the Christian also where prayer is concerned, will certainly be due to the fact that purely rationally he has had to repudiate the idea that God as an abstraction should hear prayers and answer them. Much has been written about prayer, its circumstances and forms in the various religions. In them all prayer and religion hang together most exactly. If one disregards their many differences in dogma, symbols and ritual, all religions have this in common, as William

James puts it in *The Varieties of Religious Experience*: 'Religion shall mean for us the feelings, acts and experiences of individual men in their solitude, so far as they apprehend themselves to stand in relation to whatever they may consider the divine deity.' James quotes a liberal French theologian who wrote: 'Religion is an intercourse, a conscious and voluntary relation, entered into by a soul in distress with the mysterious power upon which it feels itself to depend and upon which its fate is contingent. This intercourse with God is realized by prayer. Prayer is religion in action, thus is prayer real religion.' William James himself writes that prayer is the very essence of religion. If one accepts these philosophic reflections on the nature of prayer, one is entitled to infer that with Schweitzer, too, prayer is a necessary part of his religious life. Therefore, we also understood that he in no way dismisses divine service as valueless. In his autobiography he writes: 'The church services which I attended as a child gave me a feeling for solemnity and a need of quiet and to collect my thoughts. These I took with me out into the world and I cannot imagine existence without them. For that reason I cannot agree with those who will not let children attend the services of the grown-ups before they can understand them. Whether one understands anything or not, is not the decisive factor; what matters is to have the experience of solemnity.' This view of divine service is due first and foremost to the sermons preached by Schweitzer's father, which were full of the gospel of love and of simple, quiet devotion. 'At those times,' he writes, 'father's simple way of preaching really came into its own.' I am not sure that Schweitzer would think the same of many of the services held in our Norwegian churches. If there is to be devotion and identification, then people's mood must not be destroyed by worthless expositions of dogma and continual reminders of eternal damnation. What for Schweitzer constitutes the experience of prayer is the devotion itself, the identification, the attempt to become one with the mystical power that Schweitzer considers is implanted in all life. That this experience is of a genuinely and profoundly religious nature is proved by the fact that Schweitzer considers that through prayer he really has acquired the strength to bear the burdens of the day. It is these effects of prayer that have brought William James, among others, to the conclusion that there must be a reality behind the unknown—God or what one likes to call it—which is the cause of these effects. On the basis of his comprehensive study of prayer in the various religions he defines prayer thus: 'prayer, the inner fusing with the spirit of this world—one can call it "God" or "law"—is a process that makes real something through which spiritual strength flows causing mental and material effects in the visible world.'

*

We have made frequent use of the term 'mystical' and will have to do so again later, and it may be useful to define exactly what is meant by the term, since it is one to which so many different meanings can be given. Here, we use *mysticism* to mean a peculiar state of consciousness which is said by those who regularly experience it, to bring them into contact with a world that is otherwise not experienced by the senses. According to William James, one of the characteristics of what is known as *mysticism* is that it is a state that cannot be described,

59

but that has to be experienced, and is almost an emotional state. It also regularly provides knowledge that seems as, or more convincing that the knowledge which is acquired the reasoning intellect. If we stick to this definition, there is no doubt that Schweitzer's prayer is genuinely mystical. He has himself described the state as a sort of meditation and says that through it he achieves contact with the eternal primal force. He also maintains that through prayer he obtains a mystical strength to bear the burdens of the day. In a letter to me dated 8.5.57, he wrote: *'Beten heisst Meditation im Geiste, der sich in uns offenbart und in der Hingabe in ihm zum Frieden gelangen und zur Kraft, alles Schwere zu ertragen.'* On the other hand, there is nothing in his writings to suggest that during prayer he ever gets an increased perception of the physical or supersensual, as is often the case with the mystical identification of Christians. Even so, prayer is certainly an equally great source of strength to Schweitzer as it is to practising Christians who address their prayers to God 'in Heaven'. Schweitzer has the great advantage that, because he is an agnostic as far as world-view goes and does not expect any direct granting of prayer, he is never disappointed because prayer appears to be useless. He regularly draws strength from prayer as part of the ethical-mystical fusing with the primal cause of being and thereby achieves harmony in his whole life-view without having to compromise with his insistence on truth and honesty.

*

Another source of strength for Schweitzer is *music*—his losing of himself in Bach has been an experience that thoroughly deserves to be called mystical. We can take

it that Schweitzer feels one with the eternally unfathomable also when he surrenders to music. But his first and
greatest, continually valid source of mystical inspiration
is Jesus Christ. To understand Albert Schweitzer then,
one must learn to enter into his efforts to model himself
on Christ.

The Figure of Jesus

Like most children who are brought up in the Christian
religion, Schweitzer's attention was very early attracted
by the biblical figure of Jesus. At the age of eight he
expressed a desire for a New Testament and began
eagerly to study it. He thought a great deal about the
little baby Jesus who was laid in a crib and wondered
why the wise men from the East never bothered any
more about him. On the whole we must take it that his
need to think for himself very early brought him up
against problems that, with his insistence on truth, he
could not shirk. While he was being prepared for confirmation by Pastor Wennagel and was told that where
faith was concerned it must stand above reason, his
reaction was as he writes : 'On this point I realized that
I thought differently, despite all my respect for him. He
tried to make it clear to us that when faced with faith,
reason must be silenced. I told myself that our reasons
have been given us in order that through them we should
comprehend even the loftiest thoughts of religion. The
certainty of this filled me with joy.' Many have thought
as Schweitzer did, both before him and since, but what
is individual about him is that he could not have any
peace of mind until by exploring the best sources he
had arrived at a personal conviction of what in the Bible
was historical and what legend. As we have already

mentioned, his studies of what had been written on the life of Jesus brought him to the conclusion that the gospel of St. John is substantially made up of legend and that there is also much in the gospels of St. Mark and St. Matthew that will not stand up to scientific scrutiny. Schweitzer's picture of the figure of Jesus such as he has described it in *The Quest of the Historical Jesus,* is based on a most exhaustive study of the sources. This book, together with *Paul and his Interpreters* and *The Decay and Restoration of Civilization,* provide the basis for understanding both his view of the figure of Jesus and his elaboration of the notion of the Kingdom of God. There is no reason to go into details of Schweitzer's views here. What is of interest in connection with our subject is that he definitely repudiates the fundamental Christian dogma of the Virgin birth, Jesus as the son of God, the doctrine of the atonement, resurrection of the body and the ascension. According to Schweitzer, the main mistake of research on Jesus and the view now taken by modern theology is that it has tried to clothe Jesus' sayings in modern language, instead of interpreting them all from the basis of Jesus' own ideology of the imminent end of the world and establishment of God's kingdom (the eschatological view). In this connection he writes: 'Our Christianity is based on an illusion in so far as the eschatological expectations have not been fulfilled. On the basis of the clear statements contained in the two oldest gospels, I base this explanation of Jesus' life which I advance in opposition to the untenable one that hitherto has been accepted, namely that in all his thoughts, preaching and deeds, Jesus was actuated by the expectation that the world was soon coming to an end and that a supernatural Messianic kingdom would be founded. This is the "eschatological" explanation, which is called that because by eschatology (eschatos is Greek for "the last") is meant traditionally the Jewish-Christian doctrine of what is to happen at the end of the world.' Later on he says: 'The primitive late-Jewish metaphysics in which Jesus' conception of the world is contained makes it an unusually difficult task to give his ideas a form that is suited to our times. The task is insoluble if it is understood to mean that a detail is to distinguish between the ephemeral and the immortal. In reality there can be no question of making any such separation between the time-bound and the immortal, but only of translating the basic idea in Jesus' world-view into the concepts of our day. How would Jesus' will, direct and in its full extent, have found expression in *our* ideas and conceptions? And what form would a world-view based on that have taken, which would be so monumental and of such ethic power that it could act as the modern equivalent of the world-view that Jesus created in the late Jewish metaphysics and eschatology?' It has been one of Schweitzer's main tasks to explain to the people of today what Jesus can mean to us, if we stick to his eschatological view and do not try, as modern theology does, to make His world-concept correspond with our own. According to Schweitzer, all such attempts can only contribute to make the Jesus-figure lifeless and enfeebled. 'All attempts utterly to ignore this world-view and restrict Jesus' significance for us to his having taught us about 'God the Father' and that everyone is God's child, etc., must therefore necessarily lead to a limited and strangely colourless conception of His religion. In reality, He cannot be an authority for our understanding, but only for our will.

His mission can only be that, as a mighty spirit, He advances will- and wish-motives that we and our associates carry within us, to a height and clarity that they could not have achieved if we had had to rely on ourselves and received no impress from His personality, and that He in this way fashions our concept of the world making it in its inner essence His own, despite the difference in ideas and conceptions, and giving it the same strong appeal to ethical forces.'

The way in which we can derive benefit from Jesus' eschatological view is by working to promote 'the Kingdom of God' here on earth. Jesus' messianic supernatural kingdom must be replaced by faith and work, as a result of which this kingdom will come about if we obey the ethical instinct that is implanted in us all. 'The decisive thing about this concept of the world is the enthusiasm and heroism that wells up out of our will for and belief in the kingdom of God and which is not weakened, but on the contrary strengthened, by obstacles. A religion is capable of understanding the historic Jesus to the extent that it has a strong and passionate belief in the kingdom of God . . . If this happens, then his words are almost automatically translated into the form that they must have in *our* ideas. Much that appears initially foreign, becomes clear in its deep and eternal meaning when we fully grasp the greatness of the spirit speaking out of it. That he expected such a result brought about by supernatural ways, while we can merely conceive it as the result of moral effort, is due to the fact that our notional material has changed.' Elsewhere Schweitzer says of this conception of Jesus' preaching: 'This conception of religion and the figure of Jesus is usually brushed aside as being one-sidedly moralistic and rationalistic. The answer to this is that, when really alive and having the right intensity, it will accommodate the whole religion. For all that one can say of salvation, taking it realistically, amounts in the last resort to this, that we in an association of will with Jesus make ourselves free of the world and ourselves and win strength and peace and courage to live. Nor should one forget that Jesus himself was a moralist and rationalist who lived in the late-Jewish metaphysics. Jesus was called the Messiah, the Son of Man, the Son of God, names from the late-Jewish notional-material. For us these names have become historic symbols. That He has used them Himself is a time-related expression of His conceiving Himself as one who commands and rules. There is no name we can find that covers His personality.'

That quotation provides a clear insight of Schweitzer's views both on the task of religion and the importance of Jesus in enhancing the meaning of our lives. It will be noted that there is no question at all of building anything on Jesus' own assertion that He had come down to earth as God's son in order to expiate our sins. 'The Son of Man' is merely a name that He gave Himself and He made a mistake in thinking that the world was to come to an end and that He was to become the Messiah in the coming heavenly kingdom. We cannot base our cognition on anything that Jesus said about the supersensual. Schweitzer does not believe in the reality of any of the metaphysical speculations about Him, but, all the same, for him Jesus has not lived in vain. He stands in history as the symbol of the gospel of love and therefore He is timeless. His spirit lives and will continue to live even though He has not physically risen from the dead. If we familiarize ourselves with this idea of a future kingdom of God and comprehend the deep ethical core in it, we can strive to create this kingdom of God here on earth. It is not necessary to have dogma in order to reach this goal. 'We serve Christianity better by strongly devoting ourselves to Jesus' religion of love than by bending the knee to dogma.'

*

Schweitzer gave a special evaluation of the figure of Jesus in his thesis for his medical degree. What caused Schweitzer to choose a psychiatrical study of Jesus for the subject of his doctoral thesis was the fact that there were a number of papers that set out to show that Jesus must have suffered from some mental illness. This idea had been discussed in detail long before psychiatrists became interested in the person of Jesus of Nazareth. As early as 1835, David Friedrich Strauss in his work on the life of Jesus based on a study of the historical material, stated that Jesus suffered from a crazy idea which was that in the near future he was going to return on the clouds enveloped in a heavenly, supernatural glory and surrounded by angels, in order, as the long-awaited Messiah, to judge the world and set up a kingdom. In his thesis, *The Psychiatric Study of Jesus*, which was first published in 1913, Schweitzer takes as his point of departure three specific psychiatric works. A critical analysis of these leads Schweitzer to the result that the three authors have based their finding that Jesus was a psychopath mostly on the gospel of St. John. He then demonstrates from his own theological studies that most of the gospel of St. John, as well as some other gospel sources on which the three psychiatrists based their conclusions, are not historically valid. Thus he says on page 45, 'As far as the sources are concerned, it must in the first place be noted that the Talmud and the extra-biblical gospels—the latter are chiefly concerned in throwing light on the stories about his childhood—cannot be considered. We must also exclude the fourth gospel, for the Jesus described there is in the main—as critical research has come more and more to recognize ever since Strauss' day—a freely imagined person, the purpose of which is to improve and supplement the Jesus depicted in the first three gospels. The Jesus of the fourth gospel believes himself in agreement with Greek dogma —to be the eternal spirit of God which became flesh (Logos).' Schweitzer finds it understandable that because of these and other ideas, psychopathologists can arrive at the conclusion that Jesus must have been mentally abnormal, but he emphasizes that three-quarters of the material on which these people—Loosten, Benet-Songlé and Hirsch—base their argument comes from the gospel of St. John. The gospel of St. Luke agrees by and large with those of St. Mark and St. Matthew. But 'where it (Luke) differs from these two, it is of doubtful worth; and anyway it is of little importance for assessing Jesus and therefore can be omitted'. Schweitzer points out, however, that the accounts of Jesus' birth and childhood in the first and second chapters of Matthew are also legends and must be disregarded in assessing Jesus. Schweitzer considers the only historically reliable sources to be the gospels according to St. Mark and St. Matthew except for the first two chapters of the latter. On the basis of this material he shows that the ideas that Jesus had according to these reliable sources, and which, if taken superficially, could be used to prove that he was paranoic, nevertheless become intelligible when seen in an historical and eschatological light. Thus he points out that Jesus' idea that he was the Messiah was not so preposterous. He was said, after all, to be descended from David, and when He spoke of the Messiah coming He was putting forward the apocalyptic ideas of late Judaism. (The prophecies were that it was a descendant of David's line, living in the greatest poverty, who was to be this Messiah.) Schweitzer admits that it was peculiar that Jesus could have such ideas about himself. 'Despite it all, it is remarkable that he considered himself to be the one who was to become the supernatural successor of David's line.' And he finds that one must give up any idea of a reasonable explanation of this idea, but emphasizes that 'mere exaggeration of such an idea does not justify one in regarding it as a manifestation of psychosis'. Apart from this, Schweitzer finds support for the contention that Jesus did not develop any real mental illness: in the fact that nowhere in the reliable sources are there described any real delusions of persecution or opposition, symptoms that are always present in cases of paranoia, which he considers must have been the psychosis here, if there was one.

Otherwise, Schweitzer considers that much of the evidence on which the three psychiatrists built their case, e.g. that Jesus saw an angel in Gethsemane and the whole account of Jesus in the desert, is mere legend. A number of other points in the material which is supposed to prove Jesus' mental derangement are also unacceptable. Schweitzer's *conclusion* is that the material which the authors have taken as their evidence of Jesus' insanity is unhistorical. Besides, the authors, he says, have not understood Jesus' ideology, since they have not been familiar with its historical background. What is thus left that is historically tenable is not sufficient to prove the presence of mental disorder. His conclusion here is: 'The only symptoms that can be accepted as historic and which perhaps could be discussed from the psychiatrist's point of view, that is Jesus' over-estimation of Himself and possibly also the hallucination at His baptism, are too slender indications to be able to prove the presence of mental illness.'

This psychiatric study is a typical example of how Schweitzer went to work, when he wanted to arrive at what was historically tenable in the gospels. There is no question here of believing the gospels to be the true 'word of God'. For Schweitzer they are his source-material which has to be judged on the basis of normal scientific analysis, and, I suppose, there has seldom been a better contrast to the slavish literalism of the theologians than this little book. If Schweitzer's evaluation of the gospels is accepted, the consequences will inevitably be far-reaching. Though Schweitzer does not directly draw all the logical conclusions of his study of the gospels' description of the person of Jesus, there is no doubt that he considers that his assessment of Jesus' personality would be quite different, if the description given in the gospel according to St. John were true. Yet the gospel according to St. John is still used in our churches—as though its account of Jesus were the absolute truth, holy writ 'inspired by God', but Schweitzer thinks that the Jesus depicted there is mostly a figment of the imagination. It is evident that Schweitzer cannot bring himself to base his concept of Jesus and the Christian doctrine on anything but what his theological knowledge, his insistence on the truth and his reason will accept. A layman, obviously, cannot put forward an opinion as to whether or not Schweitzer's theological argument is tenable, but I personally have more 'faith' in Schweitzer, the researcher, than in theologians who are tied by a creed.

In his book on the search for the historical Jesus, Schweitzer states outright that we must get away from our notions of Jesus. 'We must stand free in our relation to the historical Jesus, yet at the same time be honest. We will take into consideration this historical development and rid ourselves of His notional-material, but we will bow to the powerful will behind it and try to serve both Him and our own age, in such a way that He is born anew in our time and can work to make us and the world perfect. It is this that is meant by being one with the infinite ethical world-will, and it is in this way that we become children of the kingdom of God.'

Even though Schweitzer is thus able to see Jesus' personality in an historical light without accepting him as the son of God and saviour from sin, it would give a faulty and misleading picture of his relation to Jesus were one not to emphasize that at the same time the personality of Jesus, and in particular His ethics, have been the mightiest example for him. On this point Oscar Kraus writes: 'Just as certainly as Schweitzer's ethical achievement is that most to be admired in the multiformity of his intellectual life, so is the motivation-link with Jesus which he himself is continually asserting, psychologically the most curious trait in his personality.' Even though Schweitzer is fully aware of certain defects in Jesus' personality, he has an almost mystical emotional attachment to Him. It is obvious that to a large extent he has identified himself with Him, as regularly happens when a person is intuitively impressed by great personalities. 'Jesus is of significance for our own times, because a mighty movement of ideas has its origin in Him and also flows through our age. This fact remains, no matter at what results the scrutiny of history arrives.'

When one reads Schweitzer's *Search for the Historical Jesus* and other works in which he discusses Jesus, one gets a vivid impression of the mystical attachment there is between these two personalities. One can almost speak of a dualistic attitude on Schweitzer's side, not only to the concept of God, but also to the figure of Jesus—was He God or man? Or is it not possible to explain Him? In one letter reproduced in *Denken und Tat,* he writes: 'We can find no designation that expresses His being for us.' And in the same letter he writes: 'The names used in the late Jewish material for Jesus—like Messiah, Son of Man and Son of God—have become for us historical similes. In giving Himself such titles, He was giving expression in terms of His own time to the fact that He regarded Himself as commander and ruler.' It is thus obvious that Schweitzer cannot believe in Jesus as the Son of God, yet he can find no other name that fits Him. For Schweitzer, Jesus stands for a unique, spiritually and ethically strong personality who has served him as a shining example. Consciously or unconsciously he has tried as far as he can to imitate Him in the only thing that Schweitzer considers needful where religion is concerned: to practise the gospel of love and if necessary to give his life in doing so. ('He that loseth his life . . . shall find it.') This emotional attachment to Jesus is so strong that a note of reverence appears when he describes Him in the so often quoted passage:

'As one unknown and nameless He comes to us, just as on the shore of the lake He approached those men who knew not who He was. His words are the same: "Follow thou Me!" and He puts us to the tasks which He has to carry out in our age. He commands. And to those who obey, be they wise or simple, He will reveal Himself through all that they are privileged to experience in His fellowship of peace and activity, of struggle and suffering, till they come to know, as an inexpressible secret, Who He is . . . '

It is certainly due to this mystical attachment that Schweitzer, without accepting the dogma of Jesus as God's son, can describe Him as an all but supernatural spiritual-ethical personality whose spirit still has power to lead people to try and realize the idea of the coming of the kingdom of God. It is irrelevant for Schweitzer's life-view and conception of the meaning of life whether or not Jesus is the son of God in the sense of the Christian confession. As Schweitzer sees it, Jesus' only significance for people is that through His prophecy of the coming of the supernatural kingdom of God, He has shown that love must be the driving-force, if we are to promote that which is our purpose. What matters to Schweitzer is the ideology in Jesus' life, not the reality. Jesus' gospel of love is the essential element in Schweitzer's *will-to-live*, and that again is the divine primal force that is implanted in us. Because it was first and foremost through his study of the life of Jesus that Schweitzer received his revelation of this ethical primal force, he has a mystical emotional attachment to the personality of Jesus. Jesus has inspired him to follow His example not least in self-sacrifice. Albert Schweitzer is the living proof of the fact that identification with the figure of Jesus can be the most powerful source of inspiration to ethical endeavour in a person's life, even if the link is quite independent of any belief in Jesus being the son of God. For Schweitzer, dogma was an intellectual obstacle in the way of arriving at the meaning of life. It was only when he had freed himself of it, that he was able to develop his ethical talent to the full.

Origin and Roots of Ethics

As with all religious philosophers, religion and ethics are closely coherent, where Schweitzer is concerned, but he has definitely repudiated the Christian ideology that religion stands *above* ethics and that ethics must be rooted in the one and only instance that, in the Christian view, can give it an objective formation: the transcendental deity—the absolute. In this chapter we shall first discuss his view of the basic ethical principle. In his *Kultur und Ethik* he has dealt with the question very thoroughly. As far as the origin of ethics is concerned, Schweitzer, like so many other thinkers before him, has stressed that ethics is rooted in its own human predisposition. 'Quite certainly, in one way or another, the origin of ethics is that something contained in our will-to-live is taken up and taken further by thoughtful reflection.' According to Schweitzer, the fact that man has possibilities for ethical development in itself means that he has the ability to become one with other living beings and to feel solidarity with them. On the foundation of the principle of solidarity the ethically well-developed person will act in accordance with the principle of reciprocity—will do as he will wish that others should do by him. It is obvious that Schweitzer has been greatly occupied by the purely historical development aspect of ethics. In particular, Wilhelm Stern's explanation of the essence of morality seems to have won recognition with Schweitzer. Stern wrote: 'The essence of morality is the urge to maintain life by defending it against all harmful attacks on it and here the individual experiences a feeling of solidarity with all animate beings faced with the harmful encroachment of Nature. How has this mentality come about? By the living beings of the various species through countless generations having had to struggle side by side for their existence against the powers of Nature, and in their common need ceasing to be enemies in order jointly to try to stand up to the menace of destruction or perish. This experience, which began with the lowest stage of existence, has determined the psyche of all living things. All ethics is affirmation of life determined by the idea of a common experience of the perils of existence.' In this view, Schweitzer finds support for the *sense of solidarity* with *all life* which itself comprises the ethical core of his *reverence for life*. 'The fundamental law of ethics thus is,' Schweitzer writes, 'that we must not cause suffering to any animate being, even the lowest (unless we ourselves are having to obey the principle of necessary self-defence) and that we, as far as we are able, shall be active to benefit other beings through positive action.' This *solidarity with all life* is, according to Schweitzer, something more than the herd instinct. Especially after Darwin, many philosophers have considered that the acceptance of such a biological instinct is explanation enough of the ethical predisposition. The social-medical concept of ethics is largely based on this. In order to understand Schweitzer's view of ethics one must be fully aware that Schweitzer sees the basic moral principle, that is both universal and cosmic, in just this extension of the principle of solidarity to include *all* life. It represents the mysterious, otherwise not perceptible, primal force itself.

But how is it that people, especially in the Western Countries, have advanced no further than they have in ethical development, when the basic moral principle is implanted in them? According to Schweitzer, this is because most people in these countries are passive to the ethical call and make no active effort to carry into practice that which is implanted in them. This is the main cause of the decline of Western civilization. Schweitzer has made it one of his main tasks to point out the connection that exists between culture and world-view. And since Western thought has not managed to arrive at a tenable optimistic world-view, Schweitzer has considered himself obliged to have recourse to what he calls a 'merciless showdown with western thinking'. Western thinking, he says, has not been able 'on the basis of thinking alone to base a convincing and enduring ethical world-view that affirmed both the world and life'. In practice, this means that thinking must arrive at a view of man's life that is optimistic in the sense that it finds a meaning in life as such. We shall discuss this question in greater detail in the next chapter.

For Schweitzer, *thinking* plays an essential part in ethical development. 'Something that is there already as an instinct is taken hold of by thought and by it elaborated so as to be advanced to what is perfect. In this way the role of thinking is to accomplish the affirmation of life.' It is obvious that self-analysis had much to do with Schweitzer's arriving at this point of view. We remember that he described in his autobiography how he not only directed all his thought and strength of will to implementing the ethical impulses that came to him as a sense of solidarity with his school-fellows, but also put a stop to his unethical impulses (ill-treatment of animals, jeering at the Jew Mausche, etc.) with the help of thinking and converted them into positive ethical endeavour. By his example, Schweitzer has shown— despite all the philosophizing on this question of free will—that we have the possibility of educating ourselves in an ethically valuable direction. But even though this is possible within the limits set for each individual, one cannot overlook the fact that moral development is considerably more complicated than Schweitzer seems to realize. There is, of course, a vast literature on this subject which Schweitzer does not mention and which presumably did not interest him. I am referring here to the psychodynamic processes, with identification with authoritative and collateral models, that I have discussed in my book.[1] Schweitzer obviously had great models—his father, Jesus, Bach, Goethe—with whom he has more or less identified himself, and we must believe that with him as well these models have been powerful forces in the development of his personality. Having at the same time, as is obvious, a strong will and a very definite urge to use his intelligence to work out his problems for himself as they cropped up, he has had quite unusually good conditions for developing into an ethical giant and this has made his life's work possible. But one must realize that where people with less will-power and not so great an urge to let thinking guide their lives are concerned, moral development will depend on their mental identification-mechanisms and these

[1] *Personlighets utvikling, moral og livssyn*, Oslo, 1956.

work quite automatically, without the individual being conscious of them. While ethically normal individuals are continually developing in ordinary moral milieux without thinking or the will having to play any decisive part, one is also continually seeing how an amoral milieu, e.g. a criminal milieu, develops unethical individuals through processes of identification. Where the *psychological* side of moral development is concerned, then, Schweitzer's explanation is one-sided and far from satisfactory. As has been the case with many other philosophers who have discussed this ethical problem, Schweitzer's solution is very simplified. The most important point, however, about Schweitzer's emphasis on the great importance of thinking and the will is that thereby he has made it quite clear that if the world is to advance, then these factors must come to occupy a very different and more conscious place in moral development than has been the case hitherto. We must not be content with maintaining a largely passive attitude to moral development and leaving it to mental processes that take place without our being conscious of them. We must ourselves take a hand and have *will-to-live*—that is to say the will to lead our own ethical endeavour in a direction that can advance what is the purpose of our lives, namely to let love rule among all living beings. As Schweitzer puts it: 'One real criterion of ethics is whether it allows this problem of personal morals and the problem of people's attitude to each other—with which we have to deal every day, indeed every hour, and in doing which we must become ethical personalities —to come into their own.' On the basis of this definition of the heart of the ethical problem, Schweitzer, in his *Kulturphilosophie*, counters the different philosophic

77

views of this ethical problem put forward in Greco-Roman philosophy, by the philosophers of the seventeenth and eighteenth centuries, Kant, Spinoza and Leibnitz, and at the same time he goes thoroughly into the ethics in Hegel's philosophy of nature and history. He also defines his attitude to utilitarianism and the ethics of biology and the social sciences. It is not possible here to go into details of Schweitzer's views on all these different trends in moral philosophy. Where Schweitzer is concerned, the heart of the problem is the same for all who have occupied themselves with it. He asks himself: 'What is the common good in all the multiplicity that we apprehend as good? Is there a concept of universal good? and if there is, of what does it consist and to what extent is it necessary for me? What power does it exercise over my disposition and my actions? Into what relation to the world around me does it bring me?' Put that way, the question shows the necessity of thought directing its attention to the fundamental moral principle. 'To do no more than draw up virtues and duties, is the same as to strum on the piano and think that one is creating music.' Schweitzer therefore repudiates the ethic of utilitarianism of the social sciences. It puts into people's hands the norms that are merely relative and subject to the changes of time and circumstances. That means that its stimulus on the will to the ethical can only be weak. It can even bring the will into confusion by depriving it of the elementary conviction that it has to deal in perfection without regard to given conditions and that it must fight against circumstances out of inner necessity and without knowing for certain what the result will be. After discussing the basic moral principles at which the different thinkers have arrived, Schweitzer comes to the conclusion that they are all unsatisfactory. The *thinking of antiquity* wanted to take the ethical as rational hedonism. But that becomes an egoistic utilitarianism which does not lead to an active unselfish morality. This attempt to interpret ethics as rational hedonism is not an advance, because it does not take account of altruism. But neither is *altruism*—taken in isolation—satisfactory as a fundamental ethical principle. Even if altruism is rooted in an instinct, it appears that modern thought on it has arrived at the most different and mutually conflicting conclusions. 'At one moment it is explaining that altruism is refined egoism, at the next that it is something that society forces upon the individual, and again that it is something to which society stimulates us, or, as with Bentham, that it is something the individual accepts at the urgent entreaty of society, or even that it is an instinct that he obeys. The first hypothesis is impossible; the second, third and fourth are unsatisfactory because they make the ethical out to be something that is implanted in people from outside, while the last leads into a blind alley. If altruism really is an instinct, then it must be shown how thinking affects it and can raise it up to the level of reflective-comprehending action, for only in that plane does it become an ethic. Utilitarianism does not admit this, which is its real problem, still less solve it.' Therefore, neither *striving after the rational nor self-sacrifice* can, according to Schweitzer, be accepted as fundamental ethical principles taken by themselves. He therefore raises the question whether *striving after personal perfection* can explain ethics. Plato was the West's first representative of the ethic of personal perfection and he tried to solve the problem by putting forward world- and life-negation as the actual ethical fundamental principle, as the Indians do. But, Schweitzer says, if consistently carried out this negation does not lead to ethics, but, on the contrary, invalidates it. Kant's categorical imperative, the ethic of the concept of absolute duty, does not solve the problem either. It really gives no ethical content. Nor did Spinoza nor Fichte succeed in giving ethical content to striving after personal perfection, even though they advocated world- and life-affirmation instead of life-negation.

Thus, after analysing the various attempts that have been made to arrive at the fundamental ethical principle, Schweitzer arrives at the conclusion that the solution lies in a *combination* of altruism and striving after personal perfection. To be able to understand this solution of the ethical problem, we must know something of Schweitzer's *attitude to the world-view*. Through all Schweitzer's writings, like a guiding thought, you will find that as far as world-view is concerned—that is to say the world-order and its meaning—he declares himself an *agnostic*. In *Civilization and Ethics* he says: 'The object of a world-view is to understand the meaning of everything and that is not possible for us. The greatest insight at which we can arrive through cognition is thus that the world is a phenomenon that is mysterious in every respect, is a realization of the universal will-to-live. I believe that I am the first in European thought who has ventured to admit this most depressing result of cognition and adopt a sceptical attitude to our knowledge of the world without thereby renouncing world- and life-affirmation and ethics. But even if I have renounced all idea of arriving at any comprehension of the world, this does not mean that I have irrevocably fallen prey to a scepticism the view of which is that we drift about in the world like a ship without a rudder. I merely mean that we are obliged to have the courage to look this truth in the face and that from it we must try to arrive at the valuable world-view which we feel is the correct one. Any world-view that is not based on resignation with regard to comprehension is artificial and contrived, for it rests on a false interpretation of the world. World-view means our relation to the world as it is given in our firm will-to-live when this seeks to arrive at an understanding of itself through thinking. Thus, world-view is based on life-view and not the other way round.' With this latter view Schweitzer disassociates himself radically from the Christian life-view with its interpretation of the world and all that happens in it as being the result of God's will. Whether to man's way of thinking it appears to be brutal force and senselessness or love and meaningfulness that determine people's fate, the Christian will maintain that everything has its meaning—is God's will being done. Schweitzer cannot find any such meaning in the world-order. 'The new rational thinking thus does not try to obtain certainty about the purpose of the world, a thing that is quite unobtainable. It contents itself with the fact that knowledge of the world is eternally unattainable for us humans and instead tries to arrive at an understanding of the will-to-live within us.

'Just because we are unable to understand anything of the world-order and the course of nature, they come into conflict with the mysterious ethical endeavour implanted in man. Nature knows only a blind life-affirmation.'

The will-to-live expressed in the forces of nature and in living beings strives to unfold in its entirety. But

F 81

ethical striving in man prompts him to adopt *life-negation* in order to serve other beings and protect them against hurt and destruction even by sacrificing himself. This tendency to surrender to others (in sexual impulse and love for others) is also to be found among animals; but with animals the instinct is limited to special relations of solidarity, while with people it becomes 'a permanent, rationally-based, voluntary, limitless achievement in which the individual seeks to realize a higher affirmation of life'. To explain this specifically human aspect of this surrender, Schweitzer reminds us that we must realize the importance of thinking. 'In certain ways the role of thinking is to fulfil life-affirmation. By acknowledging the life-affirmation in itself, it stimulates the will-to-live also to acknowledge and to share the life-affirmation in the multiplicity of life around it.' In order to be in harmony with the fundamental ethical principle man must employ life-negation—that is to sacrifice himself for others—as a means to fulfilment of life-affirmation. In this endeavour, however, the individual often comes in conflict with the demands made by society, since the ethics of society are in principle non-humanitarian. In order that the individual shall always decide to the advantage of society, society endeavours as far as possible to restrict the authority of the personal ethic, although it must tacitly acknowledge its sovereignty. Society wants servants who will not revolt. Even a society with a relatively high ethic is a danger for the morals of its members. And later: 'The great error of ethics hitherto has been that it will not admit the essential difference between ethical morality and the ethic that society sets up, but considers that it must and can mould both into one piece. This results in the ethic of ethical personality being sacrificed for the sake of the ethic of society. But an end must be put to this. It is essential to realize that these two forms of ethic are conflicting and that their antagonism must not be mitigated. Either the ethic of ethical personality will raise the social-ethic as far up to itself as it can, or it will itself be dragged down.'

The social ethic consists, according to Schweitzer, in society appealing to the loyalty of the individual in order to achieve what it cannot obtain by the use of laws and compulsion. It is, however, only to the extent to which society assumes the character of an ethical personality that its ethic becomes that of the ethical society. Ethics therefore becomes a very comprehensive concept: it includes as well as personal perfection through an inner liberation from the world (resignation), also active personal liberation in the ethical relation between persons and the ethic of social morality. And that brings us back to Schweitzer's attempt to solve the problem of ethics. The question is whether the ethic of altruism and the ethic of personal self-perfection can find each other and so jointly form the true fundamental moral principle. If this were to be possible, such a complete ethic could also force a decision with the social ethic. Schweitzer's view of why the world has advanced no further in ethical development than it has, must necessarily shock all who believe that dogmatic Christianity can solve this problem. To me, it is only possible to take Schweitzer as meaning that the cause of this failure to advance is the rooting of ethics *outside of being,* in the transcendental deity. As this is a very essential point in understanding Schweitzer's view of the root of ethics, let me quote the following from his *Kulturphilosophie*:

'For the ethic of self-perfection to be able to be combined with the ethic of altruism, the former must become cosmic in the proper manner. The ethic of personal self-perfection is in its whole character cosmic, since it cannot consist of anything but that man comes into a true relation to the Being in him and outside of him. The natural, outer solidarity with Being will thus be transformed into an inner, spiritual surrender to it, and the individual will let his passive or active relation to things be decided by this surrender. In this endeavour he has hitherto only reached a passive surrender to Being. The active surrender he has not succeeded in realizing. And it is this one-sidedness that makes it impossible for the ethic of personal perfection and the ethic of altruism to influence each other and jointly produce the passive and active ethic of perfection.

But why is it that the ethic of personal self-perfection never gets beyond passivity despite all our efforts? The reason is that it allows the spiritual, inner surrender to Being to be directed to an abstract concept of Being instead of to real Being. Consequently it wrongly enters into nature-philosophy.' Expressed in slightly less philosophical terms, this simply means that the fact that our ethical development has progressed no further than it is today, is, according to Schweitzer, because we have striven to make ourselves more perfect at the demand (God's commandments and other alleged transcendental revelations) of a *supra-ethical instance,* instead of obeying the demands made on us by nature and all our live fellow-creatures. By being rooted in the absolute, mysticism can no longer serve personal perfection, which is the actual profound call of mysticism. By being merged with the absolute, it becomes a goal in itself

84

which does not serve ethical development. Of this Schweitzer says: 'The ethic of personal self-perfection, which should emerge from mysticism, is thus in danger of being lost in mysticism. The tendency of mysticism to become supra-ethical is quite natural. In reality, its relationship to a quality-less and self-sufficient absolute magnitude no longer has anything to do with personal self-perfection. It becomes a pure act of consciousness and leads to a spirituality that has as little content as the presupposed absolute. Mysticism feels this weakness and endeavours to be more ethical than it is, or at any rate not to be less ethical.

'Mysticism is not the essence of ethics, but its enemy. It consumes it. And yet any ethic that is intellectually satisfying must arise out of mysticism. All profound philosophy in the last resort is nothing but a struggle for an ethical mysticism and a mystical ethic.' This brings us to another point of view that is very important in Schweitzer's view of ethics. He stresses very strongly that the Western peoples, in their endeavours to arrive at an active ethic and world-view, have been far too fearful of admitting mysticism. Our great mistake is that we have imagined that we can arrive at an intellectually satisfactory ethic and life-view *without* mysticism. This has resulted in a number of world- and life-views that certainly have had a stimulating effect, but which are neither true nor yet profound. Because of that, they are collapsing one after the other. Because they have been overfed with fictitious world-views that pretend to be the basis of an active ethic, people in Europe have no personality, no inner cohesion, nor do they feel any need of them. It is indeed high time that we abandoned this illusion. The world- and life-view of active ethics does not have any deep root in thought unless it grows out of mysticism. The problem of what we are to do with our lives is not solved just by our being hounded out into a world brimming over with the urge to be up and doing, and then not being allowed any time for reflection. Any real answer to this problem can only come from a world- and life-view that brings people into a spiritual inner relation to Being out of which a passive and an active ethic emerge as of natural necessity. The mysticism we have had hitherto has not been able to accomplish this, because it is supra-ethical. Thus, what thinking must strive to achieve is an ethical mysticism. We must raise ourselves up to a spirituality that is ethical and an ethic that includes all spirituality in itself. Only then will we be fit for life in the profoundest meaning of that word. The mysticism we have had hitherto leads to the supra-ethical, because it is abstract. But abstraction is the death of ethics, for ethics is a living relationship to animate life. Thus, we must abandon abstract mysticism and devote ourselves to a live mysticism.

'The essence of Being, the absolute, the world-spirit and all such expressions do not denote anything real, but something that is thought out in abstractions and which, therefore, it is absolutely impossible to imagine. The only real thing is Being, which manifests itself in con- crete forms of expression.'

This is blunt talk and it is impossible to misunder- stand Schweitzer where his views on the roots of morality are concerned. But while stoutly asserting that the life-views that have been put forward hitherto in western countries based on religion, including the Christian, only contain a dead ethic because they are rooted in the transcendental, he also makes it clear that the life-views that have no relation to the mystical break down too. In Schweitzer's opinion, the only solution is a mystical rooting not in an abstract, but in Being itself. This then becomes *ethical mysticism* and this in fact is Schweitzer's attempt to combine altruism with the ethic of personal self-perfection.

This solution is certainly a result of the working of the subconscious over a lengthy period. As so often happens in such cases, the answer came almost as a revelation. This was in 1915, when Schweitzer was being rowed slowly up river from Cape Lopez to N'Gomo. In the evening of the third day, as the sun went down, the phrase *'reverence for life'* suddenly occurred to him without his being prepared for it and without his having tried to find it. 'The iron door had yielded,' as he put it in his account of the event, 'the path in the thicket had become visible. Now I had found my way to the idea in which world- and life-affirmation and ethics are contained side by side.' Schweitzer's many descriptions of the concept 'Reverence for Life' make it clear that it is deeply rooted in religion. 'All the surmise and longing there is in all deep religiousness is included in Reverence for Life. But Reverence for Life not only expands all this into a finished world-view, but accepts that it has let the cathedral stand incomplete. It was only able to finish building the choir. But here, too, piety holds a never-ending service.'[1] The driving force in Reverence for Life lies in the most comprehensive and most immediate fact in our consciousness: 'I am life that wills to live, in the midst of life which wills to live.' According to Schweitzer, this motto is the point of departure for all true philosophy. 'In my will-to-live there is a longing to

[1] *Kulturphilosophie.*

go on living and to experience the mysterious consummation of the will-to-live that is called pleasure; there is, too, a fear of destruction and the mysterious restriction of the will-to-live that is called pain. So, too, it is with the will-to-live around me, either it can express itself to me or it is dumb.—Ethics thus consists in the inner urge to meet all will-to-live with the same Reverence for Life as I show my own will-to-live. This, too, is the logically necessary fundamental moral principle. Good is to maintain and promote life; evil is to destroy or repress life.' This definition, in Schweitzer's opinion, gives the ethical and absolute basic principle of good and evil, and he requires that it be carried to its logical conclusion: 'The ethical person does not ask to what degree this or that life is valuable enough to deserve compassion or to what extent it is even able to feel anything. Life as such is sacred to him. He does not snatch a leaf from a tree, does not snap off a flower, is careful not to trample on an insect. If he is working of a summer's night with the lamp lit, he will prefer to keep the window shut and breathe stuffy air than to see insect after insect fall on to his table with scorched wings. If he is walking along a road after rain and sees a worm that has strayed on to it, it will occur to the truly ethical man that the worm may dry up in the sunshine if it does not get on to earth in time and is able to bore down into it—and he will see that it does get there. If he sees an insect that has fallen into a bucket, he spares the time to rescue it with a leaf or a straw . . . Ethics is unqualified responsibility to all that has life.'

Nothing better shows the deeply religious element in Schweitzer's philosophy than this boundless respect for all life. The interesting thing is that for all that he is otherwise a rationalist, Schweitzer here goes far beyond the rational. If one imagines his reverence for life being carried to its logical conclusion, all of us, the ill as well as the healthy, would be deprived of the pleasure of having flowers in our rooms. Our houses would be alive with insects, and vermin and weeds would flourish everywhere. Nonetheless, the reverence itself compels our deepest respect for the lofty ethic on which it is based, and we can learn much from it. And why not open the window and help the fly out into the open, instead of mercilessly killing it with a swatter? And why not reverentially step out of the way of insects and flowers instead of trampling them in our path? Another question, and one of purely moral-philosophical interest, is whether Schweitzer with his 'Reverence for Life', really has managed to do what no other philosopher has yet been able to achieve, namely to arrive at the objective and absolute fundamental ethical principle. Is it really the case that all that counts as good in ordinary ethical evaluation of people's relations to each other can be traced back to the wish to maintain and promote human life materially and spiritually, while all that is accounted evil represses and/or destroys human life?

It is scarcely an absolutely tenable principle that applies to all cases and at all times. Even here there are certain eventualities, where it is not possible to avoid discussion of relative values. What, for example, must one account the highest ethical good: at all cost to maintain the life of a suffering person who, one knows for sure, is about to die, or to mitigate his suffering with analgesics even though one knows that these can reduce the length of time he has to live? And is it not a more positive ethical act to bring gladness and *joie de vivre* into a sick-room with lovely flowers than to practise absolute respect for life by leaving them to grow untouched in the field? Even though these and other examples are liable to call in question Schweitzer's assumption that with his Reverence for Life he had arrived at the fundamental ethical principle of universal application, there can scarcely be any doubt that with that concept he has given moral philosophy something that, if it were practised from the basis of the individual's will-to-live, would be a very valuable guide for ethical endeavour. One must, however, add that Schweitzer's treatment of the root of morality is faulty as far as the scientific side is concerned. This is a side of the problem on which much more light has been thrown since Schweitzer wrote about his fundamental moral principle: Reverence for Life. There are many indications that it would be possible to obtain an insight into the basic ethical problems by the study of the experience of other generations and by the scientific study of ethical values. Schweitzer has not interested himself in this aspect of the problem. That does not prevent his *Reverence for Life* being a basic principle of the utmost value.

Schweitzer writes in several places of the *self-sacrificing ethic* and life-negation as integrating factors in all ethics. By this he wishes to emphasize that if ethics is to be genuine there must be self-sacrifice. And it must be a self-sacrifice that is really felt as a renunciation of other needs that otherwise it would have been more natural to satisfy. Generosity, helpfulness, first-aid work only become ethical if they are acts that really cost something to perform. The widow who gives her mite acts more ethically than the millionaire who gives some of his surplus. That must be what Schweitzer has wanted to express with his motto: 'He who loseth his life . . . shall find it.'

What, apart from the normative side, is interesting about reverence for life as an ethical concept is that Schweitzer considers that with it he has solved the problem of combining the ethic of personal self-perfection and the ethic of altruism. As Schweitzer puts it, they become cosmic in a nature philosophy which takes the world as it is. By meeting in living surrender to living Being they both become expressions of the same inner need. Expressed in Schweitzer's philosophic terminology, this means that world- and life-affirmation are realized in life-negation. That again means that the logically necessary fundamental ethical principle runs: surrender to life is reverence for life.

It should be obvious from the foregoing that Schweitzer will not accept the idea of ethics being rooted in the transcendental. He is, of course, fully aware of the great significance of ethical values for moral development, but nowhere has he even mentioned the necessity or even desirability of these values being given by some divine authority. He is strongly influenced by the ethic of Jesus, but he emphasizes that it is not true to say that we would not have had these ethical values if we had not learnt them from Jesus—they are natural to us and arise out of the moral will. In his *Pursuit of the Historical Jesus* he goes into the question of the possible value Jesus' ethic can have for the development of mankind. He points out first that the ethic of Jesus can only be regarded as an *interim-ethic*—that is to say, that it was aimed exclusively at spiritual preparation for membership of the kingdom that was about to come and which had the ultimate purpose of fitting people to be able to stand forth as righteous on the day of judgment. This ethic, therefore, can not be of value for people today. 'It is no use trying to turn Jesus' ethic into something resembling modern social-ethics, for it is by its very nature individualistic and world-negatory and disregards all earthly conditions, but instead requires that everyone shall be made perfect within. To attempt to derive our ethic as a whole from what Jesus preached is pointless and a mistake. Jesus cannot be the foundation of our ethics, as He has been of our religion. The value Jesus has for us lies exclusively in the fact that with His ideas of the coming supernatural kingdom of God, He outlined the ethically perfect world. Jesus' great achievement is that with His natural and profound morality He conquered late Jewish eschatology and in the ideas of His day gave expression to the hope for and will to achieve an ethically perfect world. Thus, all attempts to disregard this world-view entirely and just let Jesus have the significance due to His having taught us about "God the Father" and that everyone is God's child, etc., etc., must necessarily lead to a restricted and strangely colourless conception of His religion.'

To derive benefit from Jesus' interim-ethic, then, we must free ourselves entirely from His conceptual material, yet at the same time actualize it and believe that we can realize the heart of His ethic by working 'to promote the kingdom of God here on earth'. 'The only thing that matters is that the significance of the idea of the kingdom of God for our world-view is the same as for Him, and that we experience its importance and compulsion with the same force as He,' Schweitzer writes. We have to identify ourselves with His thoughts so that there can be communion with Him. As we have already said, Schweitzer regards this communion as mystical in nature and has certainly experienced it himself in a mystical way.

In an article, *The Idea of the Kingdom of God*, Schweitzer has gone more closely into the question of how expectation of the coming of the kingdom of God, as preached by Jesus, originally made primitive Christianity optimistic in character. But, as it became obvious that the prophecy was not going to be fulfilled, the optimism gave way to pessimism. 'Because the Christians' expectations of the kingdom of God could not be fulfilled until some remote future,' he wrote, 'Christianity became a religion that no longer knew the happy temperament that characterized St. Paul and the primitive Christians. It began as a faith marked by happy expectation, but became cold and gloomy when the expectation was not fulfilled. Because of this, the idea of the kingdom of God is no longer the central one, but has been thrust into the background, and this again means that the faith has been greatly impoverished. If belief in the kingdom of God is again to acquire the importance that it had for Jesus and the early Christians, it must no longer be something supernatural, but must have intellectual and ethical magnitude. And it must not be something for which we wait, but a thing that we try to bring into being. This is the significance faith must have, if Christianity in its true character is to become what it was at the beginning, that is: a religion dominated by the idea of the kingdom of God.' One can scarcely imagine a more radical break with modern theology. The Christian faith must not be rooted in anything supernatural and certainly not stamped with belief in a future *heavenly* kingdom. The kingdom of God is our endeavouring to put into practice the fundamental moral principle that is implanted in us, and that, according to what has already been set forth, is the *will-to-live*. Thus, for Schweitzer, the concept God, according to our argument here, is to be defined philosophically as the mysterious *ethical mysticism* which he calls *reverence for life* and which itself has its origin in the fact that people have *will-to-live* among other wills-to-live.

Ethics thus has its origin in the mystical *fundamental moral principle* and this, too, is rooted in it. According to Schweitzer, this is the only absolute moral principle that can stand up to philosophical analysis. The difference from the Christian view of ethics is thus that Schweitzer's reverence for life has its origin and its field of action in man himself. Its goal is a continual endeavour to promote in man this fundamental moral principle which aims at preserving all life. The Christian ethic, on the other hand, has its origin in the transcendental.[1] And, as such, according to Schweitzer, it has its goal *in itself*. In principle, therefore, it is not ethical in nature. It is because the Christian ethic is rooted in transcendental mysticism that Schweitzer considers it of little value. 'In order to judge how ethically valuable mysticism is,' he writes, 'one must investigate its real ethical content and not just be satisfied with what it pretends or claims to contain. Do that and its ethical content proves appallingly slight, even in Christian mysticism.' He then goes on to expound, what we have

[1] To avoid misunderstanding it should be emphasized that in this book *transcendence* is only used as a term indicating the superiority of deity as opposed to *immanence*, the complete or partial identification of God with the world.

already discussed, how the decisive thing for ethics is what it is rooted in. An ethic rooted in the transcendental just becomes dead. For an ethic to be alive, it must be rooted in Being itself, and thereby the genuine ethic becomes ethical mysticism.

As has already been mentioned, Schweitzer is not content with pointing out this difference of principle between supernatural and concrete ethic. What is just as important is his forceful appeal to people that they must be conscious of the fact that this tendency to ethical mysticism is implanted in them and that they must exert their will to practise it. For, like so many other great philosophers, Schweitzer is not only a keen thinker, but he is probably greatest as a practiser of ethics.

In his *Kultur und Ethik* he has described the *practical* side of reverence for life thus: 'Open your eyes says the true ethic, and see if you cannot find a person or some philanthropic work that needs some of your time, kindliness, sympathy and effort. Perhaps there is an ill or a bitter or a lonely or helpless person to whom you can be something. An old person, perhaps, or a child. Perhaps some Relief organization is waiting for you to volunteer to give it an evening and a helping hand.' He goes on to explain how the essence of ethics is to sacrifice something of oneself. 'But along with the others one must know that our existence only acquires its true value when we experience within us part of the truth of the saying: He who loses his life shall find it.' As one sees, *in practice* there is little difference between the ethic that Schweitzer points to as the essential and that preached in our churches, but the *philosophical background* to them is radically different. Schweitzer preaches that we follow the moral need implanted in us. Our guide is not Jesus' ethic—that can no more be a basis for our knowledge than can the alleged commandments of God. If we follow the principle of reverence for life we further the purpose of life, which is to promote the kingdom of God —here on earth.

Christian theologians preach that our morality is implanted in us by a supernatural power and can be recognized as *conscience*, which they pretend to be 'the voice of God'. Their ethical norms are based on God's ten commandments. If we strive to obey them, then we are fulfilling God's will. We are to do this, not because we are thereby helping to create ethically valuable people who can create a kingdom of God here on earth, but in order to prepare ourselves for eternal life. Where modern Christianity is concerned, there is thus an egoistic motive in its ethic—that of the soul's salvation. It is, therefore, not ethical by nature. Schweitzer's reverence for life aims first and foremost at self-sacrifice for others in order thereby to create a better humanity. It is therefore essentially ethical and ought to have a prospect of becoming much more effective than the ethic based on the transcendental. It has become Schweitzer's most urgent task to awaken the West to a *new rationalism*. People must no longer remain passive to ethical thinking. 'We can no longer share the belief of previous generations that the kingdom of God will come of its own accord at the end of the world,' he writes. 'For humanity today it is a question of bringing the kingdom of God into being or of perishing. By reason of the distress in which we find ourselves we are compelled to believe that it can be brought into being and we must make strenuous attempts to do so.'

We have already mentioned how Schweitzer considers that the main reason why humanity has advanced no further in ethical development is that in the Western countries ethics have been rooted in the transcendental. Therefore we must learn from the religions of the East which base ethics on Being. But another important requirement is that people must think more and not be so passive.

III

THE REQUIREMENT OF TRUTH AND THE IMPORTANCE OF THE ABILITY TO THINK AND OF INTELLECTUAL HONESTY

WE HAVE already told how one of the traits that characterized Schweitzer even early in his childhood was his need of rational explanations of his main problems. It is remarkable that in his boyhood his thinking was not confined to purely logical questions, but that even while he was at school, he employed his thoughts on the mystical, reacting against his master's attempt to explain natural phenomena that in reality are inexplicable. Between the ages of fourteen and sixteen, this need to seek the truth through logical thinking became so urgent in him that, according to what he himself has written, he made himself a thorough nuisance to his family. 'I felt such a need to discuss things that my presence became intolerable to everyone, especially my father. I was so possessed by the idea of searching for the truth and the fitness of things that I went about in a sort of intoxication. Every topic of every conversation in which I took part had to be gone into thoroughly. Before, I had been reserved, but now I became a real disturber of the peace and ruined every conversation that had no pre-tension to be anything more than conversation. I was really quite intolerable, as intolerable as a relatively well-brought up young man can be. But it was not because I was self-opinionated, that I was like this, but because I felt a really passionate need to think and to make search along with others for what was true and fitting.'

This passionate need to seek the truth through thinking has characterized Schweitzer's whole personality ever since. Together with his innate ethical disposition and his intellectual honesty in all circumstances, it is this need that has aroused the unique admiration that the whole world feels for him.

Schweitzer's thought has been revolutionary especially in three spheres: in *theology*, where it led him to reject completely the normal Christian interpretation of Jesus' prophecy of the kingdom of God, and in *philosophy*, where he—as has been mentioned in the preceding chapter—has made a radical assault on the *western* world-view. This assault was a necessary part of his attempt to arrive at a life-view that could combine in itself the concepts of altruism and self-sacrifice, an attempt that was finally solved by his discovery of the principle which, in his opinion, is the only absolute and objectively given fundamental moral principle: Reverence for Life. Schweitzer himself considers that he arrived at this principle first and foremost by thinking. It is just in this third sphere of *ethical thought* that, in my opinion, he has made his greatest contribution as a thinker, in that he has made it clear that all thinking in the last resort necessarily leads into the irrational. At first, this may sound slightly paradoxical, but in what follows we shall see that it is quite logical and, scientifically, the only tenable attitude to the present problem: *undogmatic*, scientific research.

As far as Schweitzer's *theological* research goes, we

already know that it has led him to interpret Jesus' prophecy of the coming kingdom of God from the eschatological point of view. His thorough study of Paul was not the least of the stimuli that induced him to employ thinking also to distinguish the historical from the legendary. 'Paul has assured for us for all time the right to think in accordance with Christianity,' he wrote in his book *The Mysticism of Paul the Apostle.* 'He puts the comprehension derived from Christ's spirit above traditional belief. He has an absolute and unfailing respect for the truth. He will not hear of the servitude dictated by earlier teachers, he recognizes only that which love imposes on us. But this is not to say that he is a revolutionary. His point of departure is the faith of the primitive Christian Community, but he does not consider himself bound to halt where that stops; he maintains that he has the right to think out the thoughts dealing with Christ to their conclusion and does not take into consideration whether or not the understanding at which he thereby arrives, lies within the scope of the views ruling in the Christian Community and can be recognized as part of its faith. This is thus the first appearance of thinking in Christianity and the result gives us good reason to think that faith has nothing to fear from thinking, even if the latter troubles its peace and leads to a conflict, the outcome of which would seem unfortunate for piety.' Thus, Paul was very unorthodox and Schweitzer has consistently followed his line, irrespective of what the result might be for faith. He admits that it has caused him pain to have to break with the old, but the truth stands before him as a demand that cannot be denied. 'The prerequisite for Christianity to become a living truth in the generations to come, is,' he writes later, 'that thinkers should continually arise in it who, in the spirit of Jesus, will make belief in Him apprehendible by the ideas that belong to the world-view of the age in question.'

Schweitzer's view of the historical Jesus, together with his intellectual honesty, brought him into conflict with *Christian dogma*. He writes of this: 'We need a society, a faith and a church that respect the individual and call to life all the ethical thinking and reverence that dwells in him. On the whole, the Church tends to condemn independent thinking. Dogma has taken the place of search for the truth.' But *this is dangerous*: 'When Christianity becomes a traditional faith requiring to be accepted without more ado by every single person, it loses contact with the spiritual life of the day and loses the capacity to find new forms in a new world-view.' The truth of this cannot be contested, and it ought to be a powerful stimulus to thought not least in Norway, where a recent investigation has shown that the churches are attended by three per cent of the population.

Schweitzer's theological research necessarily led to his having to repudiate the entire Christian creed. But Schweitzer is disgusted by polemic and therefore he has never made it his *specific* task to tear down the structure of the Christian doctrine. This, however, does not prevent one seeing quite clearly that he considers most of the orthodox Christian dogma untenable, as a study of his writings, in particular his two books: *The Quest for the Historical Jesus* and *Das Abendmahl in Zusammenhang mit dem Leben Jesu und der Geschichte des Christentums*, makes obvious. Thus he writes, for example, of the *Redemption*: 'All that we can say of the Redemption amounts in the last resort to this, that we

in a fellowship of will with Jesus become free of the
world and ourselves and thereby find strength and peace,
and the courage to live.'

The idea that Jesus should suffer death to expiate our
sins is quite foreign to him and therefore he also
repudiates *communion* as a symbolic illustration of
Jesus' expiatory death. Without, as far as I can find,
ever having specifically repudiated the Christian belief
in eternal life, it is obvious from his writings that no
such belief figures in his philosophy. He has declared
himself an agnostic where world-view is concerned and
definitely repudiated the prophecy of a supernatural
kingdom to come. As far as *positive* assertions go, he has
said that we have the meaning of life *within ourselves*
and that it consists of promoting the kingdom of God
here on earth. Oscar Kraus also asserts that Schweitzer
has never said that he believes in immortality. To
Schweitzer any creation of dogma is inconsistent with
independent thinking and also quite superfluous—*the
only thing necessary* is to follow the call implanted in us
in the shape of will-to-live. In practice this means to
promote the gospel of love. Schweitzer's demonstration
of the many myths in the Bible, especially in the gospel
according to St. John, makes it quite clear that the
account cannot be historic in its entirety. If one accepts
the gospel according to St. John as being true, then both
Jesus and the disciples must have suffered from
hallucinations and delusions. This demonstration,
amongst other things, has deprived Christian dogma-
formation of its foundation and provides a model for
those theologians to follow who have the courage and
honesty to accept the requirement of truth. In this
sphere Schweitzer pays definite homage to rationalism:

'To give up thinking is a declaration of intellectual bankruptcy. When people lose faith in their ability to find the truth by thinking, they fall victim to scepticism. The living truth comes only from thinking. The mere fact of relying on being able to arrive at the truth by our individual thinking, makes us receptive to the truth. Free thought that goes deep does not lapse into subjectivism. Free thinking takes up, along with its own ideas, those that in one way or another, are valid truths of tradition and endeavours to make knowledge of them. The will to truthfulness must be as strong as the will to truth. Only an age that has the courage to be truthful can possess the truth as an inner spiritual strength. Truthfulness is the foundation of spiritual life. With their contempt for thinking, people today have lost their feeling for truthfulness and thereby their feeling for truth as well. Therefore they can only be helped by being guided back into the way of thinking. Because I am sure of this, I rise to protest against the spirit of the age and confidently take upon myself the responsibility of helping to rekindle the fire of thought.'

When Schweitzer found it necessary to take the painful course of breaking with orthodox Christian dogma, it was not only because his theological studies and his insistence on the truth prompted him to do so. The central thing in all his research and philosophy has been to find a solution of the very problem of life: why am I alive—what is the meaning of life? In this sphere, too, it was his lucid thinking that solved the problem for him.

*

As we have already mentioned, Schweitzer found it necessary to have a serious tilt at the life-view as represented in Western thought, as well as at Christian dogmatics. The *a priori world- and life-affirmation* on which Christianity builds is dishonest and rooted in *opportunistic compulsive thinking*. It is only when we have freed ourselves from this, that we can arrive at an honest life-affirmation that does not clash with our thinking. This freedom also makes it possible to combine altruism with self-sacrifice. Both are united in ethical mysticism and thus provide a possibility for a life-view based on the fundamental moral principle of reverence for life.

Schweitzer's fight to arouse the West to independent thinking does not end, however, with his exposition of a life-view on which one can build without compromising with honest search for the truth and rational thinking. He is untiring in his summons to people actively to employ their thought and will to promote the will-to-live that is implanted in us. And he feels further obliged to explain why there is no need to forgo thinking just because one is identifying oneself with all one's personality with the ethical mysticism that reverence for life involves. On this he writes in his *Kulturphilosophie*: 'Rationalism is more than a movement of thought that can be dated to the end of the eighteenth and beginning of the nineteenth centuries. It is a necessary outcome of any normal intellectual life. All real progress in the world has in the last resort been made by rationalism.' But if we are to advance, rationalism must be further employed so that we can arrive at the thinking world-view in its logical conclusion. And it is here that Schweitzer points out new ways to comprehension with the help of thinking: 'Philosophical, historical and scientific questions that earlier rationalism had not been

advanced enough to answer poured over it like an ava-
lanche and buried it. The new thinking world-view must
work its way out of this chaos. It must let reality work
on it, it must go through all kinds of reflection and
perception, it must grope its way forward to the ultimate
meaning of life and existence in order if possible to solve
some of these great problems. The ultimate knowledge,
where man comprehends his own existence in the universal Being, is said to be mystical in nature. By that is
meant that this knowledge cannot be acquired through
ordinary reflective thought, but that in one way or
another it has to be *experienced*. But why must one
assume that the path of thought ends in front of
mysticism? It is true that rational thought always halted
when it reached the borders of mysticism. It would only
go as far as it was able to put everything clearly and
logically. Mysticism, for its part, spoke condescendingly
of rational thought wherever it could, so as not to
encourage the idea that it could be forced to account to
reason. And, all the same, these two that do not want
to have anything to do with each other, belong together.

'In reason, comprehension and will that are linked in
us in a mysterious way, seek to arrive at an understanding with each other. The ultimate knowledge to which
we aspire is knowledge of life. Our comprehension
regards life from outside, our will from within. Because
life is the ultimate object for our knowledge, this ultimate knowledge necessarily becomes a thinking
experience of life. But this experience does not lie outside
the meaning of reason, but in it. Only if the will has
thought clearly through its relation to comprehension,
has an understanding with it as far as is possible, has
gone through it and has become logical in it, will it also

be in a position—as far as that is vouchsafed it—to apprehend itself at all in the universal will-to-live and in Being . . . In one way or another, by one path or another, consistent thinking thus leads to a living mysticism which is also an intellectual need that everyone has.' It is something of a feat to be able to describe so difficult a subject in such simple words as Schweitzer has done here. With this explanation he has quite simply wanted to demonstrate that, if in our thinking we do not—as is ordinarily the case—halt before the mystical problem of Being itself, but employ our will and thinking to arrive at a personal, rational world-view, then we *can* acquire personal convictions also of what is otherwise regarded as being mysticism. Schweitzer is well aware that the average person of today bothers very little about meditating on himself and the world as a thinking world-view requires. But he is convinced that man is equipped with the *potentiality* for such reflection and if this is once aroused, it will also become a need. It is remarkable that it is already more than twenty-five years since Schweitzer pointed out the necessity of thinking not being halted, when it came up against what is called the mystical. Here, as in all other questions, he is quite undogmatic and not afraid of being ridiculed by the scientists who, right up to our day, have categorically maintained an anti-metaphysical attitude where research was concerned. This problem has recently been thoroughly discussed by Arne Naess,[1] who asserts, amongst other things, that a scientist must not be dogmatic or let himself be discouraged from taking up a problem for discussion because it cannot be fitted into the methodological frame hitherto accepted by his science. New

[1] *Wie fordert man heute die empirische Bewegung*, Oslo, 1957.

problems require new methods. Schweitzer, of course, has also been a pioneer where this is concerned, amongst other things, by employing thinking also on what he calls ethical mysticism.

To be able to create cultural ideas and culture-content a world-view must, according to Schweitzer, be optimistic and ethical. This again means that the life-view must assume that one must regard the world and life as something valuable in themselves. From such an optimistic world-view there further follows a need to improve the conditions of life of the individual, of society, the nations and people in such a way that one can arrive at that which is necessary for the ultimate cultural advance: the mastery of the intellect over the forces of nature and a higher social organization. But life-view must also be *ethical*—that is to say aim at inner perfection of the personality. It is the task of thinking to work towards a world-view in which optimism—that is world- and life-affirmation—and ethics are more securely ensconced than hitherto.

*

In the previous chapter we explained how Schweitzer considers that with the basic ethical principle of Reverence for Life he has arrived at the life-view that can secure the advance of civilization. What has to happen now is that we must emerge out of the meaningless existence in which we are living and enter upon a meaningful existence: 'But there is no other way to that, than that each one individually settles accounts with himself and that we all in common ponder how our will to act and will to progress can be evolved from the meaning that we give to our own lives and life around us.'

We must not let ourselves be halted by not understanding the meaning of the world. We must recognize
that we do not and not concern ourselves with it. What
we have to strive for is to give our life a meaning from
our will-to-live as it expresses itself in us. Then life
acquires meaning *in itself*—thinking must be employed
in order to comprehend the mystical.

*

Thus Schweitzer makes it quite clear that what we need
in order to arrive at a tenable world-view is to employ
thought itself as the foundation both of life-affirmation
and ethics. Once we realize that everything revolves
round these two fundamental questions, there will be no
risk of thinking taking the wrong direction, for having
realized the relation between life-view and world-view,
thought will be in a position to unite resignation with
both world- and life-affirmation and ethics. Life-affirmation does not in fact depend on world-view to the extent
that some uncritical thinkers believe, Schweitzer says,
and that brings us again to the same point of departure
for Schweitzer's fundamental ethical principle: world-
and life-affirmation as well as ethics are given in and
with our *will-to-live*. Life-view has its roots in this
disposition that is implanted in us and life thus acquires
a meaning in itself—without it depending on world-view.
'The new rational thinking thus does not hurt the
phantom called the meaning of life. It leaves comprehension of the world alone, as a thing that will always be
unattainable for us and tries to understand the will-to-
live in us . . . of inner necessity, and in order to be true to
itself, and consistent to itself, our will to-live enters into
a definite relation to ourselves and to all the expressions

of will-to-live with which we are surrounded. And this relation is determined by reverence for life.' And thus Schweitzer's unqualified rational thinking ends in mysticism: 'I live my life in God, in the mysterious ethical God personality, which I thus do not apprehend in the world, but only experience as a mysterious will in me.'

This solution of Schweitzer's of the problem of life is radical in two ways. Compared with the Christian *a priori* thinking on the meaning of the world, that everything that happens is meaningful from the point of view of God's will and that nothing happens in a person's life that cannot be explained on that basis, his intellectual honesty and clear analysis must come as an act of liberation to most who can think for themselves and are not tied by a creed. The compulsory explaining away in hazy metaphysical terms of all the brutal and pointless things that happen, trying to make out that in spite of everything there is a meaning in everything, cannot be otherwise than hampering to the development of personality. Schweitzer openly and honestly states that he can find nothing in the world to show that God governs and directs it. The mysterious force of the deity he experiences only within himself—as will-to-live. Just as valuable as this repudiation of the *a priori* world-view is the strong emphasis he lays on the fact that, however paradoxical it may sound, all rational thinking, if carried to its logical conclusion, leads into the irrational. 'All valuable conviction is irrational,' he writes, 'and is enthusiastic in character because it cannot arise out of comprehension of the world, but has its origin in thinking experience of the will-to-live, which is the step we have taken beyond all comprehension of the world.'

Consistent rational thinking recognizes this as the truth, on and by which we must live: 'The way to true mysticism leads through rational thinking to the profound experience of the world and of our will-to-live. We must all venture afresh to become "thinking" in order to arrive at the mysticism that is the only direct and the only profound world-view. We must all go the way of comprehension up to where it passes over into an experience of the world. We must all through thinking become religious.'

To those who are not familiar with Schweitzer's expression 'will-to-live', this explanation may seem somewhat peculiar. In moral philosophy we are accustomed to use other expressions, but they are largely synonymous. Schweitzer's *will-to-live* corresponds closest to the *moral consciousness* that acts within us like a secret, autonomous authority. It bids us do what we regard as being good and is therefore in accord with the mysterious and inexplicable source of ethical endeavour. Hitherto no one has been able to provide a satisfactory explanation of this disposition in us. Neither philosophers nor psycho-analysts have been able to explain the *origin* of moral consciousness, even though we do understand a little more of the psychological mechanisms behind it. Schweitzer may therefore be quite right in maintaining that all thinking carried to its conclusion must lead into the great unknown, and as far as concerns the understanding of moral consciousness —will-to-live— in us, the term *ethical mysticism* is therefore very apt. Hitherto I, personally, have not been able to see how logical thinking can ever lead to any conclusion about what cannot be apprehended through our senses. Schweitzer has thrown light on the question for me from other angles. Most people who do not believe in a transcendental deity will no doubt be content to call themselves agnostics. Because of this very routine-thinking, which Schweitzer has shown up as typical of the West, most of us have hitherto assumed that we must either accept or reject the entire structure of the Christian doctrine. That is to say that if we join Schweitzer in admitting that we do not accept the idea of a world-order and there being a purpose to it—in other words, declare ourselves agnostics where world-view is concerned—then we must also call ourselves agnostics as far as life-view goes, that is acceptance of a meaning to our own lives. It is here that Schweitzer's philosophy can be of help to many, like he whom rational thinking has compelled to repudiate Christian dogma. But, because we have done this, there is no need to lapse into total agnosticism.

Schweitzer has shown that what is implanted in us as will-to-live has meaning in itself and connection with the mysterious primal force for which no one has yet been able to find a rational explanation. If one thinks the problem out undogmatically and with an open mind, we must come to the conclusion that Schweitzer is right: *thinking leads finally into the irrational—it becomes religious.* And there can be no doubt that it is this belief in the mystical roots of the will-to-live and the consequent positive life-affirmation that comes with it, that together have been the mainspring of Schweitzer's impressive life's work.

IV

IS ALBERT SCHWEITZER
A CHRISTIAN?

IN THE preceding chapters we have got to know Schweitzer as a radical, religious thinker for whom thinking and scientific knowledge are the ultimate guides in deciding his attitude to Christian dogma amongst other things. Jesus Christ cannot be the source of our knowledge of our religion, he writes. Even though Schweitzer has an almost mystical emotional attachment to Jesus and has been called a successor in the spirit of Jesus Christ, his writings show clearly that he does not believe in Jesus as the Son of God. Therefore he does not believe either—as has already been mentioned—in the doctrine of atonement or the sacraments, and he does not reckon with any life after this earthly one. For Schweitzer, Jesus' main importance lies in the lofty ethic that He formulated to be that which was to prepare people for the heavenly kingdom that was on the way. But this kingdom did not come, as Jesus said it would, and we have to accept that fact. In Schweitzer's opinion, Jesus' importance for us is not that He taught us about 'God the Father' or that we are 'God's children', etc., but lies exclusively in the fact that He, as a mighty, timeless and still living spirit, stimulates the will-to-live implanted in us through the overwhelming impressions we receive from His ethical personality, and thereby makes it possible for us here in the world to work for the kingdom of God that He thought had a supernatural character. As these views of Jesus' achievement also form the foundations of Schweitzer's views on religion, the latter's *only significance* according to him is that 'of being man, purely and simply man in the significance Jesus attached to that' (Schweitzer's letter to Gustav von Lüpke of June 10, 1908).

Schweitzer's philosophy is as simple as that where concerned with the essentials for man to be in harmony with the meaning that our lives have in themselves. There is no need to believe in Jesus Christ's death or resurrection, nor in eternal life or eternal damnation. According to what Max Tau wrote in the introduction to the Norwegian book, *Reverence for Life* (Oslo, 1951), Schweitzer has never submitted to a dogma. The only *redemption* necessary is to tear ourselves sufficiently free of the world to be able to practise the will-to-live that is implanted in us as a mysterious force. In order to obtain strength for serving the purpose of our lives in daily life, we must through meditation ('prayer') try to identify ourselves as far as possible with this mysterious primal force, and therein lies the significance of prayer and the source of religious inspiration to do what is good. But Schweitzer does not believe in God as a human personality whom we can expect to hear our prayers, etc. He does not believe that everything that happens in the world has a purpose, that it is 'the will of God'. He is unable to account for, in particular, all the misery there is in the world. Therefore, in Schweitzer's view, we cannot continue in a child-relationship to 'God the Father who art in Heaven'. We shall lose by giving this up, he writes to me, the comfort that lies in having such a faith. We must, first and foremost, be honest towards our own convictions; if we are, then our religion also will become purified.

*

From the theological-philosophical points of view, then, there is little point in calling Albert Schweitzer a Christian. He has arrived at his philosophy after exhaustive study, not only of the sources on late-Jewish eschatology and primitive Christianity, but also of the other great religions and philosophies. He has been powerfully influenced by Buddha who 'spiritualized the world- and life-negation and gave them a breath of the ethical', as he wrote in *Das Christentum und die Weltreligionen*. In studying the religious thinkers of ancient China, he occupied himself with the problem of the forces that rule the universe—'the pure, impersonal, spiritual principle' which these thinkers conceive as God. Ancient China was also the place where the first pacifists appeared preaching peace and love (though only about the sixth century A.D. it is true). It was these thinkers, one imagines, who inspired his idea of the *kingdom of God* to be realized here on earth. Schweitzer is fully aware of what he and we owe to them: 'Let us not try to minimise the Christian ideals that we find in non-Christians far back in time and under distant skies.' He admits that it was an experience for him to make the acquaintance of these thoughts, for spiritually they are related to Jesus' 'message of love'. But none of the oriental religions could stand up to Schweitzer's search for the truth. Most of them fail, amongst other reasons, because they are based on the illusion of a rounded-off, logical comprehension of the world. Just as, by unmasking the many myths in the Bible, he has had to repudiate

Christian dogma as it is today, so, too, he had to repudiate much in the other great religions once he had soberly analysed their content. Thus, Schweitzer has been unable philosophically to subscribe to any religion, he belongs to no confession whatever. If, therefore, by Christian is meant a person who stands firmly by the Christian creed, then it is obvious that Albert Schweitzer cannot be called a Christian. To describe him as a Christian because Jesus has been his great and most important example and because he has tried to practise Jesus' gospel of love in his work, would be justified if one means thereby that he is a typical and outstanding representative of the Christians of today.

The fact that people have disagreed so strongly and often so passionately over this question of whether or not Albert Schweitzer can be considered a Christian, is to some extent due to the fact that some lay the main emphasis on his attitude to Christian dogma, while to others 'Christian' merely means an ethically valuable person who tries to practise the essential of Jesus' gospel, namely loving kindness. Many theologians, in Norway at any rate, are contentious and will not recognize as Christians any but those who accept their own interpretation of the gospels. Of paramount importance, of course, is what Schweitzer himself thinks. He has on several occasions said that he regards himself as a Christian. In a letter to me he wrote that he regarded Christianity as the traditional ethical religion and for that reason he felt profound reverence for it, and that was why, when talking or corresponding with Christians, he used the Christian terminology (as, for example, in his Letter to a Confirmand). Against that background, then, there is nothing to be said against regarding

Schweitzer as a Christian. In fact, most people who are familiar with his ideas, his personality and life's work will consider him a shining example of the true Christian spirit. In this book, however, it is more the philosophical side of Schweitzer's philosophy of life that I have wanted to illuminate, and as far as that side of him goes, Schweitzer himself—as we have already seen —clearly realizes that he is not a Christian, but stands somewhere between pantheism and theism.

Philosophically, then, there are many labels that fit him better than 'Christian'. First and foremost he is an *original religious thinker.*

At the same time as being an agnostic where world-view is concerned, Schweitzer has advocated a reformation where thinking on the irrational is concerned. He rejects the idea of thinking in abstraction, for abstraction is the death both of religion and ethics. But all thinking must in the last resort concern itself with the mysterious irrational forces—will-to-live—that are implanted in us. Therefore, *ethical mysticism* is an apt description for his attitude to ethics and morality. The fact that Schweitzer's philosophy has met with so much admiration is due both to its philosophic content and to the fact that he has put his philosophy into practice to a greater extent than have other philosophers of equal calibre. As far as the *philosophic* content goes, its significance and the inspiration it contains lie in two particular aspects of it: in the first place, it is an expression of his absolute demand for truth and honesty, and, secondly, it allows science and reason to influence views beyond the spheres where they can be utilized for comprehension. He is fully aware that where the irrational forces in the human mind are concerned, we must bow in humble admiration before the great unknown. This is, too—in my opinion—the only scientifically tenable viewpoint. It is true that Schweitzer goes a step further than other Western philosophers, who have dealt with the same problem. He maintains that thought consciously can not only apprehend the existence of the irrational, but that we, just by thinking, are stimulated to make active use of our ethical endeavour—our will-to-live—in order to be in harmony with the actual meaning of Being. Any philosophy that is to mean anything to the individual is rooted in faith, and it is not least Schweitzer's belief in the potentialities implanted in us for promoting the kingdom of God here on earth that have caused his life-view to find an echo in the minds of so many religious seekers. His life-view is the result of original thinking, both in the religious and in the rational sphere.

Anyone who has made himself thoroughly familiar with Schweitzer's philosophy and really tried to understand this ethical giant's grasp of the basic ethical and religious problems, cannot help feeling that Schweitzer is the forerunner of a revolution that will come about in religion, ethics and thinking. What his philosophy involves, perhaps, is easier to experience than to describe. It includes much of the best in the most varied philosophies: *rationalism's* insistence on honest thinking, *Christianity's* call to charitable acts and the spirit of sacrifice, *liberal ethics'* requirement that religion and morals should be rooted in Being itself.

How is it that Albert Schweitzer's philosophy has not yet brought about any serious reformation within modern Christendom? Why do so few of our liberal theologians attribute so little of Schweitzer's views to his insistence on honesty and search for the truth? As thinkers they cannot be so very different from other ordinary educated people who find great difficulty in accepting the fantastic dogmata and the many myths in the gospel of St. John? Or is one result of the theological training to prevent independent thinking on these religious problems through expulsion or autosuggestion? An explanation and one that I know to be correct for many of the clergy, is that when faced with the 'truths' of the Bible, they stop thinking and humbly acknowledge that human thought fails when it comes to dealing with divine truths. If that is the case, then they must expect to be told that they are not honest in their religious thinking.

The only hope that, among other things, people can be stimulated to use thought to further the ethical endeavour implanted in us, lies in a new reformation in the church whereby love will come to the forefront and dogma be relegated to the background. If the view that man has the ability himself to create the kingdom of God on earth and that this is the purpose of life, could become the central theme of all religions, then people would be entitled to hope to avoid our present doom, which is to be wiped from the face of the earth. In all parts of the world, eminent thinkers are now pointing out this danger that threatens mankind as a result of having made technical development its almost exclusive goal. If mankind is to have a chance of escaping the catastrophe that threatens it, therefore, it must come to its senses and direct its endeavours to bringing about a change in the human mind itself. Many writers are pointing out that this change can only come about with the acceptance of a *new philosophy*, and many insist that there must be an end to dogmatic religious upbringing. In Norway, this view has been advocated by Wergeland, Bjornson and Nansen. Just because Albert Schweitzer is non-denominational, his philosophy and his life's work have a message to all people. His peace-call has the same background. He will remain known as a brilliant thinker and a great ethical and religious genius who, by practising his own ethical principles, has shown mankind the way it must take, if it is to reach its destination. By stressing that ethics is the primary and central factor in people's relations to each other, as well as to the great unknown, he has for all time demonstrated the only principle that is of significance for man's salvation.

Albert Schweitzer cannot be described. He must be experienced. And then he speaks to one just through the mystical contact that is the confirmation of his having touched something in one that is connected with the primal cause and object of Being itself. Schweitzer's religion consists in performing his acts of love towards all his fellow-creatures in humble surrender to the great unknown, because that is the only way in which an honest seeker after the truth can be in contact with his 'God' and thereby be in accord with the meaning of life. This is the only possible form of universal ethic and religion. There is much to indicate that the salvation of the world will depend on whether or not Schweitzer's call is going to bring about a new era in Western civilization.

GEORGE ALLEN & UNWIN LTD
London : 40 Museum Street, W.C.1

Auckland : 24 Wyndham Street
Bombay : 15 Graham Road, Ballard Estate, Bombay 1
Calcutta : 17 Chittaranjan Avenue, Calcutta 13
Cape Town : 109 Long Street
Karachi : Metherson's Estate, Wood Street, Karachi 2
New Delhi : 13-14 Ajmeri Gate Extension, New Delhi 1
São Paulo : Avenida 9 de Julho 1138-Ap. 51
Singapore, South East Asia and the Far East : 36c Prinsep Street
Sydney, N.S.W. : Bradbury House, 55 York Street
Toronto : 91 Wellington Street West